STUDIES IN ENGLISH LITERATURE NO. 59

General Editor

David Daiches

Professor of English in the School of English
and American Studies, University of Sussex

D0784660

Already published in the series:

CHAUCER: TROILUS AND CRISEYDE

by

A. C. SPEARING

*Fellow of Queens' College,
Cambridge, and University
Lecturer in English*

EDWARD ARNOLD

© A. C. SPEARING 1976

First published 1976 by
Edward Arnold (Publishers) Ltd
25 Hill Street, London W1X 8LL

Cloth edition ISBN: 0 7131 5853 0
Paper edition ISBN: 0 7131 5854 9

All Rights Reserved. No part of this publication may be reproduced, stored in a retrieval system, or transmitted, in any form or by any means, electronic, mechanical, photocopying, recording or otherwise, without the prior permission of Edward Arnold (Publishers) Ltd.

This book is published in two editions. The paperback edition is sold subject to the condition that it shall not, by way of trade or otherwise, be lent, resold, hired out, or otherwise circulated without the publishers' prior consent in any form of binding or cover than that in which it is published and without a similar condition including this condition being imposed on the subsequent purchaser.

Printed in Great Britain by
The Camelot Press Ltd, Southampton

General Preface

The object of this series is to provide studies of individual novels, plays and groups of poems and essays which are known to be widely read by students. The emphasis is on clarification and evaluation; biographical and historical facts, while they may be discussed when they throw light on particular elements in a writer's work, are generally subordinated to critical discussion. What kind of work is this? What exactly goes on here? How good is this work, and why? These are the questions that each writer will try to answer.

It should be emphasized that these studies are written on the assumption that the reader has already read carefully the work discussed. The objective is not to enable students to deliver opinions about works they have not read, nor is it to provide ready-made ideas to be applied to works that have been read. In one sense all critical interpretation can be regarded as foisting opinions on readers, but to accept this is to deny the advantages of any sort of critical discussion directed at students or indeed at anybody else. The aim of these studies is to provide what Coleridge called in another context 'aids to reflection' about the works discussed. The interpretations are offered as suggestive rather than as definitive, in the hope of stimulating the reader into developing further his own insights. This is after all the function of all critical discourse among sensible people.

DAVID DAICHES

Acknowledgements

Chaucer is quoted with line-references from *The Works of Geoffrey Chaucer*, ed. F. N. Robinson (London 1957), and Boccaccio's *Filostrato* with page-references from *The Story of Troilus*, ed. R. K. Gordon (New York 1964).

Contents

1. Introductory

Troilus and Criseyde, the greatest single work of England's greatest medieval poet, is a poem of paradoxes. A translation and yet profoundly original; a celebration of sexual love, which yet ends in sombre rejection of all human passions; a *tragedye* of the *double sorwe* of Troilus, which impresses most readers rather by its tragicomic insights into Criseyde and Pandarus; a work written for transient oral performance, yet one which finally exists as a book to be pondered by learned and thoughtful readers; a deeply secular and pervasively religious poem. *Troilus and Criseyde* embraces all these contradictions, and others, and almost no interpretative statement can be made about it that does not require correction by its opposite.

To understand *Troilus and Criseyde*, we need to begin by asking what *kind* of work it is, if only to avoid the false expectations that modern readers may bring to it, with consequent misunderstandings and disappointments. In reading a classic novel of the kind which flourished from, say, 1800 to 1950, and which is still the dominant type of fiction, we tend to be so familiar with the premises assumed by the author that we can read his work from within those premises, without even noticing that they exist. We can thus take his 'realism' for reality, and read the work of art as if it were part of the natural world. That kind of innocent reading can be highly rewarding, but it is unlikely to be satisfactory with a work written six centuries ago, on quite different premises. It will perhaps be better to approach *Troilus and Criseyde* as if it were an 'experimental' work, like *Tristram Shandy* in the eighteenth century or *Ulysses* in the twentieth, whose methods we cannot take for granted but must discover for ourselves; all the more so since it is a strongly self-conscious work, in which Chaucer frequently calls attention to his own methods, deliberately rendering his fictional illusion discontinuous, and inviting us to judge for ourselves the truth and meaning he represents or creates.

2. *Chaucer as Translator*

Like most medieval English poems, *Troilus and Criseyde* retells an existing story; and indeed, like most of Chaucer's poems, it translates a specific foreign text. Despite its Trojan setting, the origin of the love-story is not classical; it went back only two centuries before Chaucer, to the *Roman de Troie* of the French poet Benoît de Sainte-Maure. There, however, it was only an episode, as it is in Guido delle Colonne's Latin translation of the *Roman*, the *Historia Troiana*. Both these were known to Chaucer, but his main source was in yet a third language, the *Filostrato* of the Italian poet Giovanni Boccaccio, written about fifty years before the date of Chaucer's poem (1385). Boccaccio told the story of Troilo and Criseida at full length, adding the crucial figure of the go-between, Pandaro, and dedicating his work to his mistress. Chaucer probably acquired a copy of the *Filostrato* on one of his diplomatic missions to Italy in the 1370s. In translating it, he added passages from other Italian poems by Boccaccio, Dante and Petrarch, and from the Latin *De Consolatione Philosophiae* of Boethius.

Chaucer makes no claim to 'originality', and this at once undermines one modern assumption about literary works. He claims no more than that 'as myn auctour seyde, so sey I' (II.18), and he frequently follows Boccaccio very closely, turning the Italian *ottava rima* stanza by stanza into English *rime royal*. Yet he does not hesitate to change his sources, and, though without the *Filostrato* there could have been no *Troilus*, the overall effect of Chaucer's work is very different from that of Boccaccio's. Chaucer makes the lovers more modest and inhibited: Troilo had had earlier love affairs, and Criseida is franker about her own desires. It follows that Chaucer's lovers need more complicated manœuvrings to bring them together, and that Pandarus has a more significant part to play as manœuvrer; he is older than Pandaro, Criseyde's uncle instead of her cousin, and he is also more of a liar. In the *Filostrato* it is tacitly assumed that morality is a social convention based on individual hypocrisy, while in *Troilus and Criseyde* conscience is powerful and complex, and moral judgments can be made only delicately and tentatively. Even the poet's role is changed, for whereas the young Boccaccio, addressing his own mistress, claimed that 'I set down [Troilo's] sorrows and my own as well' (29), the middle-aged Chaucer wrote not as a lover but as a bookish outsider, and, being less committed to Troilus's view of things (though no less sympathetic to his sufferings), he could enter imaginatively into Criseyde's plight far more fully than Boccaccio did.

The changes made by Chaucer form a fascinating study in medieval creativity; but it would be wrong to assume that this study is the high road to an understanding of his poem. There is no reason to suppose that his divergences from Boccaccio are more significant in the overall effect of *Troilus and Criseyde* than the places where he follows him. They can scarcely have been so for Chaucer's original audience, for Italian poetry was little known in fourteenth-century England, and Chaucer could not rely on having readers who would study his poem like modern scholars, with Boccaccio in one hand and Boethius in the other. Moreover, the *fact* that the poem is a translation is perhaps more important than any specific relationship to its sources. The role of translator might seem intolerably narrow for a great poet; but the medieval translator felt free to offer an explanatory and critical running commentary on his sources. When Criseyde, after seeing Troilus ride past her window, begins to favour him inwardly, Chaucer imagines someone objecting that such love is too sudden, and proceeds to explain that this was only the beginning of love and that any suddenness showed Venus at work for Troilus. It is precisely because the translator is following a story supposed to be laid down unalterably in written sources that he is free to comment thus; and Chaucer frequently does so, defending, explaining, objecting, or regretting the ignorance in which his sources leave him on such matters as Criseyde's age and whether she had children by her first husband. The translator's situation, in fact, becomes like that of the curious observer of a real-life love affair, well-informed about some things, less so about others, inquisitive, sympathetic, gossipy. Paradoxically, then, the experience of reading *Troilus and Criseyde* may feel more like that of 'reading' life than like that of reading a novel invented in every detail by its author.

Moreover, Chaucer has at least partially fictionalized his own situation as translator. Some element of pretence is common in medieval translations: Guido delle Colonne had referred only to ancient Latin sources for his story, and had suppressed all mention of his real French source, and similarly Chaucer says nothing of Boccaccio, but asserts that he is translating 'out of Latyn' (II.14) from an 'auctour called Lollius' (I.394). Chaucer's manuscript of the *Filostrato* may have been anonymous, and he probably thought that there was an authority on Troy called

Lollius; but he certainly knew that he was not translating from Latin. He goes beyond this slight deceit into a pervasive self-dramatization as a translator who is helplessly following sources he does not understand or even approve. Thus his claim not to know whether Criseyde had children is false; Boccaccio says clearly that she had not; but once Chaucer has put forward his feigned ignorance we cannot help speculating about the matter. Throughout, the translator's comments, whether professing ignorance or offering explanation or disapproval, are part of a calculated performance, the effect of which is to draw the audience into the poem, to share in the work of creation and judgment he seems so inadequate to perform. Yet the fictionalization of the narrator-translator is not total, like that of the narrators of certain nineteenth- and twentieth-century novels—Lockwood in *Wuthering Heights*, Strether in *The Ambassadors*, Zeitblom in *Doktor Faustus*. Chaucer makes it almost impossible for us to distinguish between the performance and the reality, and this gives us further encouragement to think and feel for ourselves.

3. Poetry for Listeners

I referred to a performance intended to draw the audience into the poem; and another way in which *Troilus and Criseyde* differs from most novels is that it was composed to be read aloud. An illumination in the best of the twenty manuscripts in which the poem survives, that at Corpus Christi College, Cambridge, shows Chaucer himself reciting his work to a group of elegant courtiers, and this probably reflects the reality of medieval 'publication'. Chaucer, though of wealthy bourgeois origin, wrote for a court audience, probably including royalty at times. In 1385, Richard II was only eighteen, and his queen was younger still—'yonge, fresshe folkes' such as those addressed in the poem's closing lines. The narrator's pose of bookish inexperience must derive partly from Chaucer's relation to this courtly public, for, in theory at least, his aristocratic patrons were by definition lovers, who knew of love 'of sentement', whereas their deferential poet could only write of it 'out of Latyn' (II.13–14). In deferring to their personal knowledge, he finds another way of drawing them into the work of re-creating the old story.

As he does this, through repeated references to himself and his audience, he builds up the sense of a double reality: that of the story, so vividly evoked in the actions, words and thoughts of the characters, and that of the writing and telling of the story. The first reality is historic and pagan; the second is present and, at least potentially, Christian. The two are not held entirely separate: each penetrates the other. The medieval penetrates the Trojan, partly because Chaucer was not able even if he had wished to invent a 'Trojan' language entirely purified of the cultural and religious implications of his own time. Moreover, in order to explain to listeners pagan phenomena that add 'Trojan' colour to his story, he cannot write footnotes, but must include the explanations in the text, and thereby step outside the 'Trojan' reality. Thus Criseyde in her 'testament' bequeaths her spirit to lament eternally in a pagan afterworld, which must then be explained to medieval listeners—'the feld of pite . . . / That highte Elisos' (IV.789–90). Such minor details are symptomatic of the 'leakage' of the medieval setting into the Trojan story. Leakage in the opposite direction occurs, for example, through the Christian poet's use of literary traditions derived from classical sources, as in the proem to Book III, with its learned address to Venus and its invocation of the epic muse. The two realities, always separable, are held in tantalizing proximity throughout, until finally the Christian poet draws back from his now cheerless pagan tale into a comfortingly familiar medieval world.

Style

The tradition in which a poet addressed audiences of whom many could not read and few would ever see a copy of his work had important effects on both the style and the structure of *Troilus and Criseyde*. A poem for oral delivery, even to practised listeners, must be readily understood, for the audience cannot control the pace of reading or return to anything they have missed. The poet's style must therefore be diffuse rather than too rich and concentrated. The diffuseness of *Troilus and Criseyde* cannot easily be illustrated briefly, for it pervades the whole poem. One has only to compare it with later long poems, such as *Paradise Lost* or *Hyperion*, to see how little concentrated its normal style is: it is notably *not* a work in which every rift is loaded with ore. That is one reason why twentieth-century literary criticism, devised to deal with concentrated, deeply-textured literature, makes so little immediate impression on it. The most concentrated literary device, and one widely seen in our century as the very essence of poetry, is the metaphor; yet Chaucer manages almost entirely without original metaphors, and when he does use them it is with great caution. For instance, 'a cloudy thought' is a relatively simple metaphor, in its implicit equation of inner experience with the weather. It is used by Chaucer to describe Criseyde's mood as she tries to decide whether to allow herself to love Troilus, but only after lengthy preparation:

> But right as when the sonne shyneth brighte
> In March, that chaungeth ofte tyme his face,
> And that a cloude is put with wynd to flighte,
> Which oversprat the sonne as for a space,
> A cloudy thought gan thorugh hire soule pace,
> That overspradde hire brighte thoughtes alle. . . .
>
> (II.764–9)

To enjoy that beautiful passage, one must adjust oneself to the leisurely pace of the fourteenth-century listener.

Another example of extended, leisurely comparison occurs in the scene in Book III, relating the first consummation of Troilus and Criseyde's love. What is being described is an experience of exceptional intensity, as charged with sensation and emotion as any of which human beings are capable. It might be thought that the natural way to describe it would be to use an intense, charged, loaded style; but that is not Chaucer's way. Here too he writes diffusely, employing a series of similes, each fully developed in its own terms (III.1226–47). First he compares the embracing lovers to honeysuckle twisting round a tree; then Criseyde to a nightingale which is first frightened but then sings out loudly; lastly Troilus to a man being led to execution who is unexpectedly rescued. The passage embraces a wide range of experiences—birds, trees, plants, shepherds, approaching death, a sudden rescue—but with easy deliberation, giving us time to take in all their implications. There is no question of finding in *Troilus and Criseyde*, as in Shakespeare's mature work, line after line in which language is used in a completely original way, with an unparalleled immediate richness of meaning. In Chaucer, meaning emerges gradually from the juxtaposition of largely familiar phrases.

It is not that Chaucer objects to compression in itself. There is nothing wrong with a metaphor, however compressed, so long as it is already part of the common language, and therefore quickly grasped by a listener. *Troilus and Criseyde* is full of pithy phrases which are metaphors in that they imply a comparison of one realm of experience with another; but they were nearly all part of the English language in Chaucer's time, and are often enough part of it now. Some samples: 'He was tho glad his hornes in to shrinke' (I.300); 'For love bigan his fetheres so to lyme' (I.353); 'Now artow hent, now gnaw thin owen cheyne!' (I.509); 'Stond faste, for to good port hastow rowed' (I.969); 'she hath now kaught a thorn, / She shal nat pulle it out this nexte wyke' (II.1273–4); 'Pandare . . . / Felte iren hoot, and he bygan to smyte' (II.1275–6); 'Or casten al the gruwel in the fire' (III.711); 'It is nought good a slepying hound to wake' (III.764); 'But kanstow playen raket, to and fro, / Nettle in, dok out, now this, now that, Pandare?' (IV.460–61); 'For thus men seyth, "That on thenketh the beere, / But al another thenketh his ledere"' (IV.1453–4); 'Pipe in an ivy lef, if that the lest!' (V.1433)

One critic has described Chaucer as a poet who seems 'to extend our consciousness, to increase its powers of observation and sharpen its capacity for delight, without revealing anything new to us, and without even making us look at things in a new way.'[1] Chaucer is usually willing to rely on common, traditional wisdom, on what 'men seyth'; though it must be added that, with both common sayings and written sources, it is difficult to determine the point at which a genuine reliance on authority passes into an excess which is allowed to provoke doubt in the audience's minds. Pandarus especially is a great relier on proverbial generalizations, and their wisdom can sometimes seem painfully inapplicable to specific situations. 'The newe love out chaceth ofte the olde' (IV.415), though a true enough observation in general, offers no comfort to Troilus, whose love is a total commitment quite out of the common run. We are incited to doubt the adequacy of worldly wisdom; and thus, though Chaucer's use of language may not reveal anything new to us, it does make us look at things in a new way—each in his own way.

Conversation

A high proportion of *Troilus and Criseyde* consists of conversation, and its style generally includes much that is conversational, easy and unpretentious. In medieval courts, conversation, especially about love, was a favourite activity and art. One of the first things Criseyde asks about Troilus when she learns of his love for her is, 'Kan he wel speke of love?' (II.503) A poem about love might appropriately emerge as a development out of courtly conversation. A small example of how Chaucer catches in his verse the very note of conversation about love is the scene where Pandarus finds Criseyde and her ladies having a poem read aloud to them (an encapsulation within the poem of its own manner of delivery):

[1] John Bayley, *The Characters of Love* (London 1960), p. 68.

> Quod Pandarus, 'Madame, God yow see,
> With al youre fayre book and compaignie!'
> 'Ey, uncle myn, welcome iwys,' quod she;
> And up she roos, and by the hond in hye
> She took hym faste, and seyde, 'This nyght thrie—
> To goode mot it turne—of yow I mette!'
> And with that word she doun on bench hym sette.
>
> 'Ye, nece, yee shal faren wel the bet,
> If God wol, al this yeer,' quod Pandarus;
> 'But I am sory that I have yow let
> To herken of youre book ye preysen thus.
> For Goddes love, what seith it? telle it us!
> Is it of love? O, som good ye me leere!'
> 'Uncle,' quod she, 'youre maistresse is nat here!'   (II.85–99)

There is no difficulty whatever in the language of that passage, and not a phrase that might not have been used in real conversation. Chaucer's skill is to deploy word and gesture so as to crystallize the whole social scene, in which simple words have manifold delicate human implications. This is lighthearted conversation in which the tone is set by the presence of ladies; conversation between Troilus and Pandarus is equally colloquial, but often less playful and more outspoken; conversation between the lovers is different again.

The words of conversation may be simple, but their implications are frequently complex. One common element in conversational language is a kind of significant imprecision, intolerable in prose. It may involve ambiguity of reference, or perhaps running together two different constructions, so that one statement changes almost imperceptibly into another in mid-sentence; and there are many other kinds of imprecision, which form important parts of the way conversation conveys meaning and emotion. Chaucer is highly sensitive to these significant imprecisions, and often uses them in *Troilus and Criseyde*. An example of imprecision of reference occurs when Pandarus is trying to persuade Criseyde to visit his house; in fear of scandal, she asks if Troilus is there, Pandarus falsely assures her that he is not, and Criseyde agrees to come, urging him to

> 'Loke al be wel, and do now as yow liste.'
>
> He swor hire yis, by stokkes and by stones,
> And by the goddes that in hevene dwelle,
> Or elles were hym levere, soule and bones,
> With Pluto kyng as depe ben in helle
> As Tantalus!   (III.588–93)

A powerful way of swearing 'yes'—but 'yes' what? It is not clear whether Pandarus is swearing yes, he will 'loke al be wel' (and again, it is unclear what that would mean), or yes, he will do as he pleases. The ambiguity is deliberate; it forms part of the rich haze of uncertainty in which the characters' motives and intentions are enveloped throughout the poem.

An example of imprecision of construction occurs later in the same book. Pandarus has hastily thrust the fainting Troilus into Criseyde's bed, in order to revive him. Troilus recovers, but

> Soone after this, though it no nede were,
> Whan she swiche othes as hire leste devyse
> Hadde of hym take, hire thoughte tho no fere,
> Ne cause ek non, to bidde hym thennes rise.
>
> (III.1142–5)

Is Chaucer simply informing us that Criseyde found it unnecessary to make Troilus leave her bed once he had recovered, or is he explaining why she found it unnecessary—because there seemed nothing frightening in his presence, or no danger of anyone knowing about it? It does not exactly mean any of these things, but slides about meaning none of them and all of them. Our daily conversation is full of such imprecisions, but Chaucer is one of the few poets who have been able to make use of them to convey, precisely, mixed and imprecise motives—here, not only in Criseyde, but in the narrator who is attempting to explain the motives which could justify a fact that evidently shocks him.

Definition and Formality

By contrast, some of the poem's spoken language, especially in moments of self-discovery, has a precise definition which stands out sharply against the more usual indefiniteness. There is, for example, Troilus's response to Pandarus's suggestion that he should turn his love elsewhere after Criseyde has left Troy:

> Thow biddest me I shulde love another
> Al fresshly newe, and lat Criseyde go!
> It lith nat in my power, leeve brother;
> And though I myght, I wolde nat do so.
>
> (IV.456–9)

Or Troilus's agonized acknowledgment that Criseyde has finally abandoned him, and that, even so, he cannot stop loving her:

I se that clene out of youre mynde
Ye han me cast; and I ne kan ne may,
For al this world, withinne myn herte fynde
To unloven yow a quarter of a day!
In corsed tyme I born was, weilaway,
That yow, that doon me al this wo endure,
Yet love I best of any creature!

(V.1695–1701)

It is not by accident that such painfully exact statements of the total and permanent commitment involved in love come from Troilus. His unbreakable *trouthe*, when it is forced to realize itself, demands a ruthlessly definite language, whereas a sliding idiom is more appropriate to Criseyde, who is 'slydynge of corage' (V.825), and to Pandarus, who is hardly less so.

Moreover, an important element in the poem's language is not conversational at all. Chaucer was well acquainted with Latin models of formal style, in classical and medieval authors, and with the systematic treatments of stylistic elevation in rhetorical textbooks. His interest in such literary theory is shown by his use of a large vocabulary of literary terms belonging to medieval *ars poetica*, such as *matere* (I.53, etc.), *digression* (I.143), *prolixitee* (II.1564), *abregge* and *diffusioun* (III.295–6), *encresse* and *dymynucioun* (III.1335). The stylistic range of *Troilus and Criseyde*, from realistic conversation to the ringing oratory of some of the proems and the 'Swich fyn . . .' and 'Lo here . . .' stanzas of the conclusion, is extraordinarily wide. It was Italian poets such as Boccaccio and Dante, writing a language still closely related to Latin, who had shown the possibility of achieving in a modern vernacular a 'high style' comparable to that of classical Latin poetry. The poetic language of Chaucer's proems, with their Latinate constructions and word-order, and rhetorical devices such as the sustained invocation of Venus in the proem to Book III, shows a particularly strong Italian influence. Alongside them may be set the ornate *chronographiae*, formal markings of time and season which bring mythological and astronomical learning to bear on the common experience of passing time.[2] Before Chaucer, there had been no writing in English at once so elevated and classically learned, so melodious and flexible. The coexistence within the poem of many different styles, often sharply differentiated and not merging one into another, has the effect of making us aware of all styles as conventions,

[2] See I.155–8, II.50–56, III.351–4, 1415–20, IV.225–9, V.8–14, 1016–22, 1107–10.

alternative artistic choices, rather than as mere reflections of an unquestionable reality.

Structure

Writing in a tradition of oral delivery also had important effects on the structure of *Troilus and Criseyde*. A poem of such length must inevitably have been read aloud in instalments. That, no doubt, is a major reason for its division into five books, marked off by proems each including a classical invocation. The resulting structure is similar to that of a television serial, in which each episode must represent a new beginning, to take account of the possibility that some listeners will miss an episode or two, and the probability that the audience will need time to become properly attentive when each episode begins. This is not an uncommon kind of artistic structure; it is also found in nineteenth-century novels written for serial publication. But it was particularly common in the Middle Ages, when Romantic conceptions of works of art as 'organic' were unknown, and there was a general preference for sectional structures. We find many paintings divided into separate wings, related together, certainly, in shape, colour and meaning, but each within its separate frame. An extreme example is Van Eyck's *Adoration of the Lamb*, with its many separate leaves; a less extreme one, produced for the late fourteenth-century English court culture in which Chaucer wrote, is the Wilton diptych. Here one wing shows the Virgin and Child surrounded by angels, the other Richard II with his patron saints. The two wings are strongly linked in colour, and they make up a single meaning composed of interrelated gestures and symbols; but they create separate imaginary spaces, and occupy separate frames. Medieval cathedrals, too, are divided into separate sections—nave, aisles, transepts, chancel—each experienced as an independent space, though together they form a single building.

Some recent scholars have seen the architectural analogy as a key to the structure of medieval poems. Professor R. M. Jordan claims that there is a distinctive 'Gothic' aesthetic, with a theological basis in medieval ideas about the geometrical structure of the universe: 'The typical Chaucerian narrative is literally "built" of inert, self-contained parts, collocated in accordance with the additive, reduplicative principles which characterize the Gothic edifice.'[3] *Troilus and Criseyde* is certainly composed as a series of self-contained scenes, though it also has a strong narrative impetus, which drives from scene to scene. The parts are self-contained, but hardly

[3] *Chaucer and the Shape of Creation* (Cambridge, Mass. 1967), p. xi.

inert: sparks of energy are constantly flying across the gaps between them.

The opening offers a simple example of sectionalization. The first proem does not flow organically into the main narrative, but is explicitly separated from it, not just typographically (as in a book for readers) but in the actual words. After indicating his subject, invoking Thesiphone, and inviting prayer for unhappy lovers, Chaucer brings this introduction to an end, and tells us that what follows is the *materia*, the actual story:

> Now herkneth with a good entencioun,
> For now wil I gon streght to my matere,
> In which ye may the double sorwes here
> Of Troilus in lovynge of Criseyde,
> And how that she forsook hym er she deyde.
>
> (I.52–6)

After this, the *materia* itself is broken upon into a series of distinct scenes, with the joints not usually concealed but deliberately made visible. Hence we find explicit transitions such as 'Now lat hire slepe, and we oure tales holde / Of Troilus . . .' (II.932–3), or 'Now lat hire wende unto hire owen place, / And torne we to Troilus ayein . . .' (III.218–19). The development of each scene on its own terms between such transitions is not a mere concession to the brevity of the listeners' attention-span; it makes possible emotional effects of great power and importance. Thus each scene can represent the characters' feelings and intentions at a particular moment extracted from the inexorable temporal flow of the narrative. At the end of Book IV, when the lovers are about to part, we know (because it is laid down in the old books) that Criseyde will not keep faith with Troilus. But Criseyde does not know this; she really intends to return, sees Troilus's forebodings as mere *fantasies* (IV.1615), and even urges *him* not to be untrue to her. It is no case of simple hypocrisy or shallowness: she really means it, and, because her intentions are insulated from the outcome by the independence of the scene, we feel not contempt or knowing superiority but genuine pity. It is like seeing in old photographs 'a past that no one now can share / No matter whose your future'.[4] The past exists in its own integrity, alongside what has succeeded it, and no less valid.

A further effect of scenic independence is to make possible thought-provoking uncertainties. What happens in the poem happens in the stable and isolated present of a specific scene; 'development' and change are generally seen to have occurred only in retrospect. A striking example is

[4] Philip Larkin, 'Lines on a Young Lady's Photograph Album'.

indicated by Criseyde when she is first in bed with Troilus, and he urges her to yield to him. She answers, 'Ne hadde I er now, my swete herte deere, / Ben yold, ywis, I were now nought here!' (III. 1210–11) We see that this must be true; but when exactly was the moment of yielding? We cannot tell: it seems to have happened in one of the gaps between scenes (perhaps after Criseyde awoke from her dream in Book II?) rather than in any specific scene. Similarly, we do not know exactly when Criseyde decided not to return to Troy, nor when Pandarus stopped thinking that she would return: at V.355 he assures Troilus with apparent sincerity that 'She nyl hire heste breken for no wight', while at V.505–8 he privately dismisses Troilus's hopes of her return with a contemptuous 'Ye, haselwode!' Not to know such things is once more to be in the position of a curious observer of real life, with only intermittent access to others' thoughts. Thus the scenic discontinuities of Chaucer's Gothic narrative paradoxically produce an effect more lifelike than we can find in the continuous and omniscient analysis of many 'realistic' novels.

The sectional structure of *Troilus and Criseyde* further involves the splitting of scenes themselves into semi-independent subsections. In Book I Chaucer inserts into Troilus's solitary lamentation a song he composed about his love. Chaucer begins telling us about this at line 389, and then inserts a whole further stanza introducing it, in a way which deliberately breaks continuity within the scene, and makes us aware of the song as an artistic unit in its own right:

> And of his song naught only the sentence,
> As writ myn auctour called Lollius,
> But pleinly, save oure tonges difference,
> I dar wel seyn, in al that Troilus
> Seyde in his song, loo! every word right thus
> As I shal seyn; and whoso list it here,
> Loo, next this vers he may it fynden here.

> (I.393–9)

(Chaucer here has in mind a reading as well as a listening public, a point I shall take up shortly.) There are many less obvious cases of sections which exist at least semi-independently of the scenes in which they occur. In Pandarus's speech in Book II persuading Criseyde to respond to Troilus's love, there are stanzas on the traditional *carpe diem* theme at lines 344–50 and 393–9, in which we seem to hear not Pandarus's voice so much as that of a long literary tradition of persuasions to love. At III.988–1050 Criseyde addresses to Troilus a lengthy speech on jealousy; this is directed to its context, and indeed causes him to swoon; but it is surely developed far beyond what the context requires, or what might be thought in keeping with the level of realism of the scene to which it belongs. A more notorious case is that of Troilus's soliloquy on predestination (IV.958–1078), a Boethian insert whose separability from the main body of the poem is unmistakable, for it is omitted from some manuscripts and added later to others. It may be helpful to think of such speeches or parts of speeches as analogous to operatic arias, arising out of a dramatic context but elaborated as units which make no pretence of being organically linked with the narrative continuum.

A final example of sectionalization may be found at the poem's close. Here there is an obvious determination to break continuity, as Chaucer passes successively from the narrative to Troilus's failure to kill Diomede in battle, to an address to ladies, to an address to his own 'litel bok' (1786), to a resumption of the narrative, telling of Troilus's death and ascent to the heavens, to an address to 'yonge, fresshe folkes' (1835), to further reflection on the substance of his story, to an address to Gower and Strode, to a dedication to the Christian God. As the poem approaches its end, the sections become briefer, and we become increasingly conscious not of the organic unfolding of the story, but of the artistic activity of the poet, adding one fragment after another to his mosaic, and changing from one perspective and one tone to another. It is a passage of great emotional power, depending on subtly-varied discontinuity, as past and present, pagan and Christian, nostalgic tenderness and doctrinal rejection, are alternated with cunning restlessness, to find rest at last in a mercy which embraces both story and listeners.

As we look back over the poem, we can see that its discontinuities and apparent casualness do not imply carelessness or lack of advance planning. Chaucer clearly envisaged not only an immediate audience of courtly listeners, whose first demand was for entertainment, but also a reading public who would see the work in manuscript, and be in a position to view it more critically as a whole. He addresses not only 'ye loveres that ben here' (II.1751) but also 'Thow redere' (V.270); and, as the pile of written pages gets thicker, the sense of the poem's existence as a book, not a mere text for performance, becomes more important, until eventually he can address it as such—'Go, litel bok, go, litel myn tragedye' (V.1786)—and hope that scribes will copy it accurately. He is the first English writer to envisage his work as having a future existence and as belonging, however humbly, to a classical tradition alongside the great writers of the past. In Book III he had submitted to the 'correccioun / Of yow that felyng han in loves art' (III.1332–3), but in the penultimate stanza he offers the poem for correction not to these courtier-

lovers but to the learned writers Gower and Strode. This shift in emphasis
is itself likely to have been premeditated. Chaucer seems generally to
have followed Pandarus's advice about construction:

> For everi wight that hath an hous to founde
> Ne renneth naught the werk for to bygynne
> With rakel hond, but he wol bide a stounde,
> And sende his hertes line out fro withinne
> Aldirfirst his purpos for to wynne.
>
> (I. 1065–9)

Pandarus applies the building analogy to the planning of a love affair; but
in its original source, a medieval Latin work on the art of poetry,
Geoffroi de Vinsauf's *Poetria Nova*, it is applied to the planning of a poem.
Chaucer's unexpected insertion of it into *his* poem is evidence enough
that he took its message seriously. We nowadays come to *Troilus and
Criseyde* as readers, and in some ways that puts us at a disadvantage; but
we have to deal with a poet who, though he could not foresee the
multiplication of printed copies of his work, did write for future readers
as well as for contemporary listeners.

4. Romance

If, in order to know what to expect of it, one asked what kind of work
Troilus and Criseyde is, the short answer would be that it is a romance.
That would be an unsatisfactory definition in many ways, for 'romance'
was not the name of a specific genre in the Middle Ages: it probably
meant nothing more exact than a narrative written in the vernacular
rather than in Latin. We can be somewhat more exact by calling it a
courtly romance—one written for an upper-class audience, such as that at
Richard II's court, and appealing to the interests of such an audience
(which would not exclude the possibility of a critical treatment of their
own values). One consequent characteristic of courtly romance is that its
characters are themselves aristocratic. *Troilus and Criseyde*, unlike many
novels, makes no attempt to give a picture of society outside a narrow
aristocratic circle. Troilus is a king's son, Pandarus is a member of the
Trojan ruling circle, Diomede claims to be 'As gentil man as any wight

in Troie' (V.931), and, although Criseyde is the daughter of a treacherous priest, Chaucer raised her from the lower social status in which Boccaccio had placed her, and she clearly leads a life of easy leisure. For such people, economic constraints hardly exist: as Troilus assures Criseyde, if they ran away together,

> I have kyn and frendes elleswhere
> That, though we comen in oure bare sherte,
> Us sholde neyther lakken gold ne gere.
>
> (IV.1521–3)

Thus class and money, two central concerns of the classic English novel, have no place in Chaucer's poem. Yet high social rank brings other constraints, such as the concern with reputation which is a major factor in preventing the lovers from eloping; and not even the great are exempt from the turns of Fortune's wheel, or from infidelity, or from death. The grandeur of Criseyde's palace only intensifies its desolation when she has departed.

The central characters of courtly romance are normally youthful. In *Troilus and Criseyde* Chaucer treats age with unusual realism: his ignorance of Criseyde's age allows us to speculate that, as a widow, she may be beyond her first prime; and Pandarus, her uncle, seems to be distinctly older than she and Troilus, though he behaves as one of the younger generation. Still, youth predominates; and its life is treated in an idealizing way. The lovers are beautiful, and they are described in superlatives which the poet fully endorses. Of Criseyde he tells us that

> As to my doom, in al Troies cite
> Nas non so fair, for passynge every wight
> So aungelik was hir natif beaute,
> That lik a thing inmortal semed she,
> As doth an hevenyssh perfit creature,
> That down were sent in scornynge of nature,
>
> (I.100–5)

and Troilus is described by Pandarus as one

> In whom that alle vertu list habounde,
> As alle trouth and alle gentilesse,
> Wisdom, honour, fredom, and worthinesse.
>
> (II.159–61)

Idealization is a fundamental characteristic of medieval romance, in which it further differs from the novel; though of course medieval people well knew that noble birth does not guarantee noble behaviour, and many romances represent the failure of noble young people to live up to the ideals which provide patterns for their lives.

The chief themes of romance correspond to the activities which, in theory at least, were characteristic of the young aristocracy—love and war, activities corresponding also to two fundamental instinctive drives, sexual and aggressive, and therefore of permanent interest. The medieval aristocracy was by origin a warrior-class, and it was martial prowess that ultimately justified its existence. And, as has been said, courtiers were lovers and experts on love almost by definition. Love is usually seen in courtly romances as a higher value than war: the hero must possess prowess, but its purpose is to win his lady's love. The social justification of prowess is normally omitted, but *Troilus and Criseyde* is somewhat unusual in putting warfare in a political setting. Behind the individual activities of the knights lies the struggle of Troy and Greece, and we see unusually clearly the necessity of the warrior-virtues to defend the besieged city. But even so, Troilus's skill and courage 'for the townes werre' (III.1772) are seen primarily in a personal light, for 'this encrees of hardynesse and myght / Com hym of love, his ladies thank to wynne' (III.1776–7). It is evidently his rash anger in battle, caused by his misery at Criseyde's unfaithfulness, that causes his death; but there is no suggestion that he is behaving irresponsibly towards his society. Warfare, indeed, is subordinate in *Troilus and Criseyde*. Chaucer's undertaking is to write not of 'The armes of this ilke worthi man, . . . / But . . . Of his love' (V.1766–9), and, though the siege is always a threat in the background, he generally hurries over military details. Our closest glimpse of Troilus as a warrior shows him not fighting but riding back from a victorious skirmish, modestly blushing.

5. *Aspects of Love*

Love and Religion

Love is the central theme of *Troilus and Criseyde*, from the introductory section, where the word *love* and its derivatives are used thirteen times in eight stanzas, down to the mention of love—now that of Christ—in the very last line. While it would be misleading to claim love as a medieval invention, the Middle Ages was probably the first period in which love was seen as the central and most important experience of human life. 'The highest concern of all creatures is to love and be loved,' wrote a fifteenth-century English hermit.[1] From the eleventh century onwards, love becomes a major theme of both secular and religious writings: God's love for man and man's for God is seen as the motivating force of Christianity, and lyrics and romances of love between man and woman spread across western Europe. The religious emphasis on love, and the fact that in Chaucer's time the most sensitive and passionate treatments of love in English came from devotional writers such as Richard Rolle and Walter Hilton, are factors to be remembered when we consider the use of a religious language of love in *Troilus and Criseyde*. For Troilus, as for many earlier heroes of romance, love comes as an experience of religious intensity, and one that is described in religious terms.

While jeering at lovers in the temple for their 'lewed observaunces' (I.198) (which already suggests that love is a religion), he is struck with an arrow from the God of Love, who is angry at this blasphemy. Cupid and his arrows belong to a literary convention going back to classical times; but, within the pagan setting of the fiction, this god may be thought as real as the others the Trojans worship. The arrow corresponds to a glance from Criseyde's eyes, which has a profound effect, arousing

> So gret desir and such affeccioun
> That in his hertes botme gan to stiken
> Of hir his fixe and depe impressioun.
>
>   (I.296–8)

He continues, for appearances' sake, to keep up his jeering at love's *ordre* or *lay* (I.336, 340)—terms normally used of the religious orders of medieval Christianity—but he has in fact undergone a conversion: 'Blissed be Love, that kan thus folk converte!' (308) Within this religion, salvation lies in union with the beloved lady; and, like Christian salvation, it cannot be won by right, but only granted by the lady's free mercy. So Troilus finds on the night of his love's consummation: 'Here may men seen that mercy passeth right' (III.1282). Through Criseyde's mercy he gains his heaven, and 'in this hevene he gan hym to delite' (1251). Returned to earth, he can thank Pandarus for his help, in having 'in hevene ybrought my soule at reste / Fro Flegetoun, the fery flood of helle' (1599–1600). Later it seems that his religion has been false—'farwel

[1] Richard Methley, *Scola Amoris Languidi*, opening sentence quoted by David Knowles, *The Religious Orders in England*, II (Cambridge 1955), p. 224.

shryne, of which the seynt is oute' (V.553)—its scriptures no true gospel—'God wot, I wende, O lady bright, Criseyde, / That every word was gospel that ye seyde' (V.1264–5)—and he enters a kind of hell.

And yet what relation does the pagan lovers' heaven bear to the Christian heaven believed in by Chaucer and his audience? From one point of view it is a dangerous snare, a blasphemous parody. So, when the narrator exclaims of the lovers' first night together, 'Why nad I swich oon with my soule ybought, / Ye, or the leeste joie that was theere?' (III.1319–20), his words, though not his intention, include the meaning that the price of such bliss is the loss of one's soul. Thus, by the end of the poem, Troilus's love can be seen as part of those 'payens corsed olde rites' (V.1849) that are to be rejected. From another point of view, the religious language of love is a mere *façon de parler*, used as easily by the cynical Diomede as by the sincere Troilus. When Diomede assures Criseyde that 'I am nat of power for to stryve / Ayeyns the god of Love, but hym obeye / I wole alwey' (V.166–8), we know well enough that it is his own appetite he obeys. From a third point of view, the application of religious terms to human love is a witty game. This possibility is suggested from the very beginning, when the narrator classes himself as a mere servant of the servants of the God of Love, and we recall that one of the Pope's titles was *servus servorum Dei*. He proceeds to beg lovers to pray that 'Love' may bring those in Troilus's situation 'in hevene to solas' (I.31), and that 'God' may grant those 'That ben despeired out of Loves grace' a quick death (40–42). It seems impossible to disengage a single strand of serious meaning from this witty tangle; and we continue to find daring jokes based on the parallel between the religion of love and Christianity, with *its* 'God of Love'. Thus the narrator comments on Criseyde's pretended anger at Pandarus's role in getting her into bed with Troilus, 'What! God foryaf his deth, and she al so / Foryaf, and with here uncle gan to pleye' (III.1577–8). And Pandarus seems about to invoke the Christian God (of whom he knows nothing), and is then made to correct himself:

> Fil Pandarus on knees, and up his eyen
> To heven threw, and held his hondes highe,
> 'Immortal god,' quod he, 'that mayst nought deyen—
> Cupid I mene—of this mayst glorifie.'

> (III.183–6)

None of these perspectives on religion and love can be seen as expressing the poem's total view. The link between human love and religion is not *merely* one of literary convention, blasphemous parody, social custom, or daring humour. In Book III, particularly, the love of Troilus and Criseyde is evoked with joyful and compassionate tenderness, as an experience of incomparable meaning and importance. Chaucer has written perhaps the most powerful sustained description of sexual love in English, and no single 'point of view' will serve to lay bare the essential structure of an experience which includes (among other things) shame, timidity, aggression, surrender, absurdity, worship, desire and content. It transcends all other experiences open to most human beings; and for it the transcendent language of religion is truly chosen. What the poem recurrently affirms is, in the words of Malory's Maid of Astolat a century later, that 'all maner of good love comyth of God.'[2] Since its characters, unlike the Maid, are pagans, they cannot assert as she does that no offence is done to the Christian God by earthly love; but that God is repeatedly seen as the source of all loves. He is the 'auctour . . . of kynde' (III.1765), and love is a universal impulse in the nature He created. With Troilus's very first glimpse of Criseyde, we are warned that

> evere it was, and evere it shal byfalle,
> That Love is he that alle thing may bynde,
> For may no man fordon the lawe of kynde.

> (I.236–8)

Even Pandarus inists that love is universal, though it may fall into different categories:

> Was nevere man or womman yet bigete
> That was unapt to suffren loves hete,
> Celestial, or elles love of kynde.

> (I.977–9)

Spiritual love and natural love are both love. The proem to Book III forms an extended invocation and celebration of love. This 'love' is eventually named as 'Venus' (48), but the name is not meant to restrict the poem's scope to pagan loves, for an earlier stanza has identified God's love with the attraction that pervades the created world:

> In hevene and helle, in erthe and salte see
> Is felt thi myght, if that I wel descerne;
> As man, brid, best, fissh, herbe, and grene tree
> Thee fele in tymes with vapour eterne.
> God loveth, and to love wol nought werne;
> And in this world no lyves creature
> Withouten love is worth, or may endure.

> (III.8–14)

[2] *The Works of Sir Thomas Malory*, ed. E. Vinaver (Oxford 1967), XVIII.19.

Although this invocation is largely translated from Boccaccio, Chaucer
has transferred it from Troilus (who might be suspected of exaggerating
love's power) to the narrator, and given it its authoritative position as
proem. And whereas Boccaccio had referred only to the pagan gods,
Chaucer added the emphatic line, 'God loveth, and to love wol nought
werne.'

Having moved that speech, Chaucer had to find new material for
Troilus's song at the end of Book III. He had already made him, when
first embracing Criseyde, address love as 'thow holy bond of thynges'
(III.1261), and even cry, 'O Love, O Charite!' (1254), identifying human
and religious love. Now he constructed a new song for him, derived
from Boethius's De Consolatione. The song—'Love that of erthe and se
hath governaunce' (III.1744–71)—presents love as ruling both earth and
heaven, sustaining both the order of nature and the human 'couples' who
'dwelle' in 'vertu' (III.1749), and as deriving from God, for it is 'his bond'
(1766). When Criseyde is about to be parted from Troilus, she also has
some telling remarks about the love that has bound them. Significantly,
she has rarely used religious language about love, though she saw the
imminent parting as a fall from heaven into hell (IV.712–13). Now she
does not see love in philosophical terms, or speak of it as divinely
ordained; but she does present their love as eminently *natural*:

> To what fyn sholde I lyve and sorwen thus?
> How sholde a fisshe withouten water dure?
> What is Criseyde worth, from Troilus?
> How sholde a plaunte or lyves creature
> Lyve withouten his kynde noriture?
>
> (IV.764–8)

Even at the end, where the concept of an all-embracing cosmic love
seems to have been shattered by an ascetic Christian distinction between
the love of God and 'blynde lust' (V.1824), human love retains
suggestions of the natural, in the address to the folk who are young and
fresh (like plants or flowers), and in whom love 'up groweth' (V.1836).
In 'This world, that passeth soone as floures faire' (V.1841), the growth
and decline of love are still seen as part of a God-ordained natural order.

'Courtly Love'

Much modern discussion of *Troilus and Criseyde* has assumed that it is a
poem about 'courtly love', by which is generally meant a rigid and
artificial system of behaviour, thought to have been prevalent in

medieval courtly life and reflected in courtly literature. This system is usually supposed to derive from two medieval texts—the *De Amore* of Andreas Capellanus and the *Roman de la Rose*—though the most influential exposition of 'courtly love' is far more recent: that of C. S. Lewis, in *The Allegory of Love*. Recent studies have cast doubt on these suppositions;[3] and I hope it has emerged from the foregoing discussion that it is misleading to describe Chaucer's poem as being 'about courtly love' in any more specific sense than that it is about the love of courtly people. It is better seen simply as a poem about love, though love modified by customs and assumptions that we may find strange. Chaucer reminds us that 'for to wynnen love in sondry ages, / In sondry londes, sondry ben usages' (II.27–8). We may need to learn about the *usages* of Chaucer's time, but it is still love that is to be won and lost: a permanent human impulse, though differently channelled by different cultures.

One consequence of the existence of love as an instinctive drive which is also an experience of central intensity and importance is that its subjective and objective faces often differ. The subjectivity of love is fully realized in *Troilus and Criseyde* through Chaucer's subtle and tender realization of the consciousness of his characters, for whom their own experiences must be of unique and absorbing significance. But we also glimpse them from the outside, following with almost comic predictability an age-old pattern. When Troilus writes to Criseyde in Book II, for all Pandarus's advice about epistolary style, his letter comes out just like all other love-letters:

> First he gan hire his righte lady calle,
> His hertes lif, his lust, his sorwes leche,
> His blisse, and ek thise other termes alle
> That in swich cas thise loveres alle seche.
>
> (II.1065–8)

And later too we are told that he 'dide also his other observaunces / That til a lovere longeth in this cas' (II.1345–6). Indeed, one effect of the conception of love as an *ordre* with its *observaunces* is to emphasize that, to an onlooker, lovers are as much alike as the birds that sing in the springtime—'So priketh hem nature in hir corages' (*Canterbury Tales* A.11). The juxtaposition of subjective and objective views of love can cause amusement, but it can also produce painful clashes of perspective.

[3] See *The Meaning of Courtly Love*, ed. F. X. Newman (Albany 1968); J. M. Steadman, '"Courtly Love" as a Problem of Style,' in *Chaucer und seine Zeit*, ed. A. Esch (Tübingen 1968); E. T. Donaldson, *Speaking of Chaucer* (London 1970), ch. 11.

When Criseyde leaves Troy, Pandarus urges Troilus to find another lover, asking him, 'Artow for hire and for noon other born? / Hath Kynde the wrought al only hire to plese?' (IV.1095–6) That Nature urges promiscuity is one of the arguments of the *Roman de la Rose*, the supposed textbook of 'courtly love'. It is *human* nature that demands the fidelity that is Troilus's highest virtue.

Idealization and Feudalization

The idealization which is part of romance in general naturally affects its treatment of love. Love is seen first as an emotion aroused by a woman in a man, leading him to idealize her as his superior. It is *his* emotional experience rather than hers that is the subject of poetry, and Chaucer undertakes 'The double sorwe *of Troilus* to tellen . . . In lovynge' (I.1–3). Chaucer's remarkably feminist poem also enters deeply into Criseyde's feelings, but those feelings involve notably less idealization of Troilus. She generally retains a certain coolly judicious self-possession. When she sits alone, after seeing him ride past, she considers whether or not to fall in love (Troilus never supposes that he has the option of not loving her); and her contemplation of his merits is surprisingly objective:

> And eke I knowe, of longe tyme agon,
> His thewes goode, and that he is nat nyce.
> N'avantour, seith men, certein, he is noon;
> To wis is he to doon so gret a vice;
> Ne als I nyl hym nevere so cherice
> That he may make avaunt, by juste cause;
> He shal me nevere bynde in a swich a clause.
>
> (II.722–8)

Criseyde goes on to remind herself that Troilus could have any woman in the city as his love, 'For out and out he is the worthieste— / Save only Ector, which that is the beste' (739–40). It is impossible to imagine Troilus inserting such an afterthought, and thinking of Criseyde as the *second* most beautiful woman in Troy. On the contrary, once he has seen her, his only doubt is whether she is a woman or a goddess, and he immediately dedicates himself to her service:

> But wheither goddesse or womman, iwis,
> She be, I not, which that ye do me serve;
> But as hire man I wol ay lyve and sterve.
>
> (I.425–7)

The terms *serve* and *man* indicate a feudalization of the love relationship: the lover becomes his lady's vassal, and she becomes his 'mistress' quite literally. His submission is all the more striking in a prince, to a woman who, though certainly a lady, is his social inferior. When Criseyde agrees to 'Receyven hym fully to my servyse' (III.161), she stipulates that

> A kynges sone although ye be, ywys,
> Ye shal namore han sovereignete
> Of me in love, than right in that cas is.
>
> (III.170–72)

Suffering and Death

Love is associated not only with submission but with suffering, sickness and death. If to fall in love is to be 'thorugh-shoten and thorugh-darted' (I.325), the wound is bound to cause pain; and Troilus first expresses his love with sighs and groans (I.360). His love is 'his sorwe' (I.390), and his song is a Petrarchan exploration of the paradoxes of a love which is also pain, a 'wondre maladie', a 'quike deth' (I.419, 411). Love, as in many courtly romances and lyrics, is experienced as a kind of secular passion: the greater the suffering, the truer the love. Troilus is seen as a sick man, in need of medical aid, first from Pandarus, but ultimately from Criseyde herself. When Pandarus promises his help, Troilus

> . . . fareth lik a man that hurt is soore,
> And is somdeel of akyngge of his wownde
> Ylissed wel, but heeled no deel moore.
>
> (I.1087–9)

It is no mere metaphor. When Pandarus arranges for the first meeting of the lovers in Deiphebus's house, his excuse for Troilus's presence is illness, and Troilus comments that feigning is unnecessary, for he is 'sik in ernest' (II.1529). His use of 'termes of phisik' (II.1038) in his love-letter has been fully justified; and meanwhile Criseyde thinks, 'Best koud I yet ben his leche' (II.1582). No comment is needed on the sickness to which Troilus reverts when Criseyde leaves Troy, a sickness at first imaginary (V.617–27) and then so real that he needs a crutch (V.1219–25). As the metaphors of so much courtly poetry again turn literal, his life becomes no less nightmarish than his dreams, and the spectacle arouses pity and horror.

Similarly with the association of love with death. As soon as Troilus has seen Criseyde, he asserts that if she shows no pity he will lose not only 'hele and hewe' but life itself (I.461–62). Pandarus conveys this message, with the addition that, 'if ye late hym deyen, I wol sterve' (II.323). At their first meeting, Pandarus once more urges her 'that ye han on hym routhe, . . . and doth hym nought to deye' (III.122–3); and, when Criseyde spends the night at his house, he assures her that if she refuses to see Troilus till next day, she will 'putte his lif al nyght in jupertie' (III.868, 877). She agrees to see him, and, when she takes seriously his supposed jealousy, he feels 'The crampe of deth to streyne hym by the herte' (III.1071), faints, and is thrust into bed with her by Pandarus. The second phase of his 'double sorwe' is also frequently associated with death, and Troilus more than once contemplates suicide, notably when Criseyde swoons and he thinks her dead (IV.1156–90).

Two aspects of this persistent association of love with death call for comment. The ultimate death of Troilus can come as no surprise: his love, like Romeo's, has been 'death-marked' from the beginning, and the period of happiness between his first and second sorrows has seemed a mere interlude. (Indeed, Chaucer dramatizes it as a single night, though he adds briefly that 'many a nyght they wroughte in this manere' (III.1713), and we later learn that the affair lasted for three years (V.8–14).) Troilus's life has been a mere rehearsal for death, so that death, when it comes, even so senselessly, is felt as a fulfilment, and the contempt Troilus expresses from the heavens for all earthly things, though shocking, is also a logical culmination of his living dedication to death. There is deep feeling in the invocation of death which is his response to the exchange of prisoners:

> O deth, that endere art of sorwes alle,
> Com now, syn I so ofte after the calle;
> For sely is that deth, soth for to seyne,
> That, ofte ycleped, cometh and endeth peyne.
>
> (IV.501–4)

The self-contempt which prevented him from daring to disclose his love now returns in a more numbing form—'for tyme is that I sterve, / Syn in this world of right nought may I serve' (IV.517–18)—and the dissolution of the self in death becomes a natural conclusion to its dissolution in love.

The other noteworthy aspect of the association of love with death is its effect on the lady. Her lover is entirely at her mercy, and she apparently has a freedom of choice denied to him. Thus Criseyde tells herself that a

> . . . man may love, of possibilite,
> A womman so, his herte may tobreste,
> And she naught love ayein, but if hire leste. (II.607–9)

But her very power over him can be used as a weapon against her, because, if she is not heartless, it lays her open to almost irresistible moral blackmail. She is repeatedly told that Troilus will die if she does not take pity on him; and, for rather implausible good measure, Pandarus will die too. When Troilus first disclosed who it was that he loved, Pandarus assured him that, because she was virtuous, 'So foloweth it that there is som pitee' (I.899) in her. Her genuine pity for Troilus's genuine sufferings helps to convert her power into weakness. To show *pitee* or *routhe* can mean many things; and Pandarus determinedly uses the ambiguity in the courtly language of love to urge her from kind words to the gift of her body. Of course, her own instincts are involved too; but she does not show the frank eagerness of Boccaccio's Criseida. Chaucer sees with great penetration into the secret vulnerability of a woman in such a situation, and, as she pities Troilus, so he pities her.

Secrecy

I turn now to another of the poem's assumptions about love: that it should be secret. This assumption is shared by all the characters, from the moment when Troilus conceals his first response to Criseyde, and determines to tell no-one of his 'love that oughte ben secree' (I.744). Paradoxically, it is the need for secrecy that makes it seem impossible to both lovers that they should elope in order to avoid separation. But, it may be asked, why did they not marry, since both were free to do so? Some reasons why are implied in the social situation depicted, for Troilus is a prince, who would scarcely be permitted to unite himself publicly with the daughter of a notorious traitor to his city. But there is no suggestion in the poem that the lovers would have wished to get married if they could. The situation is not like that in *Romeo and Juliet*, where the young couple's desire for open marriage is thwarted by their families' enmity. In *Troilus and Criseyde*, on the contrary, it is taken for granted that, barring any external interference, they will go on being secret, unmarried lovers for ever.

But why so great a concern for secrecy? Though they are pagans, this must be partly a matter of Chaucer's projection back into the fictional past of medieval assumptions that sexual relations outside marriage were sinful. But there is no suggestion in the descriptions of lovemaking in the poem, explicit as they are, that there is anything specifically sinful about this love, between these people. There are inhibitions to be overcome, but not a breath of the pornographic pleasure in actions felt to be shameful in themselves. The wish for secrecy has not a merely negative origin, in Christian asceticism; secrecy is felt to be desirable in itself. One reason for this must be that secret experience is intenser and more fully personal than experience which is public. The lovers are more fully united in sharing what is known to no one else. But in *Troilus and Criseyde* secrecy is not consciously enjoyed as an additional relish to sexual pleasure, as it is in the *Filostrato*, where Criseida tells Troilo that 'Our love, which gives thee such pleasure, does so because thou must needs act warily and but seldom come to this delight. But, if thou hadst me at thy will, the glowing torch that now kindles thee and likewise me, would soon be quenched' (89). Chaucer's lovers are more innocent than that. They are children of an age which was first discovering the delights of private and personal experience, when such experience was still difficult to obtain. In the early Middle Ages, nearly every aspect of life was collective, from worship to sleep. From the eleventh century onwards, we find the development of private religious devotion, based on a personal and secret love relationship between the soul and God, and frequently using the language of sexual love; at the same time, we find the emergence of courtly romance, with its personal and secret devotion between man and woman; and somewhat later, the development of physical arrangements for the wealthy to eat and sleep in private. We may less emphasize the secrecy of love because we are used to living private lives; we may even find exhibitionism more exciting. In Chaucer's time, privacy was newer and rarer. One reason why so much of the poem's action—and not only its sexual action—takes place in bed must be that only there could privacy be obtained. The medieval aristocracy had the leisure to cultivate their emotions, and they were also more likely to possess the physical arrangements, such as private chambers, trapdoors and curtains, which made secret relationships possible. But private experience must have been all the more precious to them, because so much of their lives was lived in public. When Criseyde merely spends the day with her uncle, she takes a whole train of ladies with her, and that is one reason why Pandarus has to make such elaborate arrangements to bring Troilus to her in secret. Private experience is pervasively contrasted with public, as a privilege which may also be an agony (as when Criseyde's friends congratulate her on being about to rejoin her father, and wrongly imagine that her tears are because she must leave *them*). Hence a public, social scene must be developed around the worlds of private experience; and I shall return to this later.

There is an obvious paradox in the public recitation of a poem about a secret love affair. Chaucer could have suppressed this paradox, by assuming for his narrator—like the authors of many novels—a Godlike omniscience. But he does not usually do this: as we have seen, his narrator emphasizes that his knowledge of the story comes from 'Lollius', not from personal experience. This emphasis creates a curious double perspective in the scenes of greatest intimacy, such as the great love scene of Book III, where events and feelings are described as if by an eyewitness, yet there are frequent reminders that this is only a translation from old books—reminders which momentarily dissociate us from the fictional illusion and bring us back to the poet and audience who are involved in creating that illusion. Thus, when Troilus plucks up courage to clasp Criseyde to him, Chaucer writes:

> What myghte or may the sely larke seye,
> Whan that the sperhauk hath it in his foot?
> I kan namore, but of thise ilke tweye,—
> To whom this tale sucre be or soot,—
> Though that I tarie a yer, somtyme I moot,
> After myn auctour, tellen hire gladnesse,
> As wel as I have told hire hevynesse.
>
> Criseyde, which that felte hire thus itake,
> As writen clerkes in hire bokes olde,
> Right as an aspes leef she gan to quake. . . .
>
> (III.1191–1200)

How did the ancient scholars come to know about Criseyde's response? Such intrusions are not naïve or inadvertent, for Chaucer is not aiming at the deception of an unbroken illusion, but at bringing into his poem a critical awareness of its own nature. He deliberately raises the paradox of secrecy in such a way as to bring it to the audience's attention. The poem includes several discussions of the need for secrecy, and one of the most interesting occurs in Book III, before the love scene. Pandarus begs Troilus to preserve Criseyde's reputation, 'For that man is unbore, I dar wel swere, / That evere wiste that she dide amys' (III.269–70). Among the courtly listeners, however, there can be few who do *not* know that she 'dide amys'; and, in order to avoid seeing this paradox, the audience would have to forget their own presence as intrusive overhearers of this supposedly secret conversation about secrecy. Pandarus shudders at the possibility that anyone should know how *he* has behaved in bringing the lovers together, yet this is a secret to which all of us, listeners and readers, are inevitably party. At times, Chaucer almost seems to make Pandarus aware of the presence of his large audience, as when he politely explains to Troilus that his remarks about the folly of boasting are not meant for him personally but 'for foles nyce, / And for the harm that in the werld is now' (III.324–5). Since only Troilus is present within the poem to hear these remarks, they must be directed at the fools among the poem's audience. Finally, Troilus reminds Pandarus of his reluctance to tell even him of his love for Criseyde, and asks, 'How dorst I mo tellen of this matere, / That quake now, and no wight may us here?' (III.370–71) Even the dullest listener would recognize that he himself was hearing the very words in which Troilus is saying that only Pandarus could hear him. Thus the paradox of secrecy points to the problematic nature of fiction itself.

Honour

A related value of great importance in Chaucer's treatment of love is honour, or, as he usually calls it, *name*. Already in Book I, though Pandarus is eager to help Troilus gain Criseyde's love, he begs him to 'Requere naught that is ayeyns hyre name; / For vertu streccheth naught hymself to shame' (I.902–3). Pandarus returns to the same theme in the scene I have just been discussing. He defends his own motives in acting as a go-between: he has acted from friendship, not for money; and he reminds Troilus that 'the name as yet of here / Among the peeple, as who seyth, halwed is' (III.267–8). What people think about her is evidently as important as what she really is; and sometimes this concern for reputation can seem half-comic, as when Pandarus threatens Criseyde that he and Troilus will both commit suicide. The appeal is not only to her pity but to her concern for 'What men wolde of hit deme' (II.461) if Pandarus really cut his throat before her. Like her *pitee*, Criseyde's concern for her *name* can be used as a weapon against her, and Pandarus is not slow to exploit it. When she declines to receive Troilus's letter, Pandarus thrusts it into her bosom, with a challenge: 'Now cast it awey anon, / That folk may seen and gauren on us tweye' (II.1156–7). And similarly, when he brings Troilus to her bedroom, he reminds her of the damage an outcry might do to her reputation: 'Lat no wight risen and heren of oure speche. . . . They myghte demen thyng they nevere er thoughte' (III.756, 763). In such cases it is impossible to tell what relative weight is to be given to Criseyde's care for her *name* and her secret desire for Troilus; but it is clear that she is vulnerable, and is under real pressure from her uncle.

Later her deep-rooted anxiety about what 'men' may 'deme' has more serious implications. Among all the motives that lead her to reject Troilus's pleas that they should elope rather than be separated, fear of what people would say about them both is crucial. Thus she argues passionately and at length:

> They wolden seye, and swere it, out of doute,
> That love ne drof yow naught to don this dede,
> But lust voluptuous and coward drede.
> Thus were al lost, ywys, myn herte deere,
> Youre honour, which that now shyneth so clere.
>
> And also thynketh on myn honeste,
> That floureth yet, how foule I sholde it shende,
> And with what filthe it spotted sholde be,
> If in this forme I sholde with yow wende.
> Ne though I lyved unto the werldes ende,
> My name sholde I nevere ayeynward wynne.
>
> (IV.1571–82)

Troilus himself cares deeply about Criseyde's reputation, and he has earlier put to Pandarus very similar objections to the proposal that he should abduct her:

> Yet drede I moost hire herte to perturbe
> With violence, if I do swich a game;
> For if I wolde it openly desturbe,
> It mooste be disclaundre to hire name.
>
> (IV.561–4)

Thus it is not surprising that, for all his misgivings, he bows to her argument.

It may be difficult for us to recognize the genuine importance of this ideal of reputation—*name*, *honour*, *honeste*—for the aristocratic society of Chaucer's time. Perhaps people nowadays are unwilling to acknowledge how far their sense of their own identity depends on their sense of how others see them. In literature, the ideal goes back to earlier heroic poetry, such as the *Chanson de Roland*, where the thought of what others would say about cowardice is a prime motive in ensuring that warriors act courageously. But in courtly romance *name* was not accepted so uncritically as it had been earlier. Values were internalized; and several fourteenth-century English romances, among them *Sir Gawain and the Green Knight*, postulate a gap between reputation and the underlying moral reality. One can be too much concerned with one's *name*, too little with one's true nature. The pressures on a woman to preserve her reputation for chastity were doubtless even stronger than those on a man to preserve his for courage and integrity; yet *Troilus and Criseyde* is perhaps the only English romance which seriously explores a woman's dilemma in this respect. Criseyde's concern for her reputation is increasingly, yet always compassionately, called in question, until eventually she loses her reputation in seeking to preserve it.

This paradox is underlined by a powerful irony, which, like much in the poem, forces us to think about its own existence. Poetry is one of the chief means by which *name* is preserved. It is books which have transmitted Criseyde's name from the imagined Trojan past to Chaucer's present; and the irony is that it is not her *name* in the sense of good reputation that has been carried down, but her *shame*, as the best-known of all unfaithful women. In a moment of painful insight, Criseyde herself foresees this:

> Allas! of me, unto the worldes ende,
> Shal neyther ben ywriten nor ysonge
> No good word, for thise bokes wol me shende.
> O, rolled shal I ben on many a tonge!
>
> (V.1058–61)

If she had been less concerned about her *name*, and therefore more willing to risk elopement, she would have avoided this everlasting *shame*; yet then presumably none of 'thise bokes'—Chaucer's sources, and his own poem—would have been written.

Trouthe

What Criseyde eventually loses her reputation for is not primarily chastity, but *trouthe*. This too she foresees—'Allas! for now is clene ago / My name of trouthe in love, for everemo!' (V.1054–5)—and Troilus laments: 'Allas, youre name of trouthe / Is now fordon' (V.1686–7). But *trouthe*—fidelity, integrity, trustworthiness—is not, like *name*, a variable and socially-determined quality, but is personal, internal and permanent. Trust, the basis of friendship, is much invoked when Pandarus is trying to persuade Troilus to confess whom it is he loves, for, as he says, 'to trusten som wight is a preve / Of trouth' (I.690–91). Still more than friends, lovers are committed to each other in *trouthe*, and so, at a moment of pathos and dramatic irony on their first night together, Criseyde begs Troilus, 'Beth to me trewe, or ellis were it routhe; / For I am thyn, by God, and by my trouthe!' (III.1511–12)

While the lovers are together, *trouthe* can be taken for granted, but once they are parted it becomes one of the poem's central questions. It first emerges as such in Troilus's answer to Pandarus's suggestion that he should find another mistress. Pandarus, he says, is asking him to 'traysen hire that trewe is unto me' (IV.438), and that is impossible, 'For, Pandarus, syn I have trouthe hire hight, / I wol nat ben untrewe for no wight' (IV.445–6). And towards the end, when Criseyde's falsehood has become manifest even to Troilus (whose *trouthe* makes it hard for him to see *untrouthe* in others), he speaks repeatedly of *trouthe*. He wishes that 'syn ye nolde in trouthe to me stonde' (V.1679), at least she would not make false promises. If Criseyde is untrue, 'Who shal now trowe on any othes mo?' (V.1681; cf. 1263); why does not God, 'that oughtest taken heede / To fortheren trouthe' (1706–7), punish this offence? For Troilus, the specific event opens up general metaphysical problems. And these provide a link between the pagan story and its Christian conclusion. Troilus is an *exemplum* of *trouthe* itself, totally committed to Criseyde once he loves her, and unable to 'unloven' her (1698) even when he knows she is false. And it is in his *trouthe* that he comes nearest to the Christian God, who 'nyl falsen no wight' (1845), and one of whose names is Truth. Whatever the ultimate destination of Troilus's soul, it is surely his *trouthe* that fits him for the vision from the heavens in which he comes closest to the Christian perspective of Chaucer and his audience.

The opposite of *trouthe* can be called *untrouthe* or treachery or betrayal; and it is through this complex of meanings that the poem's foreground theme of love and its betrayal is connected with its background theme of treachery. Criseyde is the traitor Calchas's daughter, and he is defined in terms that would equally apply to her: 'hym that falsly hadde his feith so broken' (I.89). Again, the Trojan prisoner for whom she is exchanged, Antenor, is unimportant in this particular story, but his name was famous with medieval audiences, for he was the traitor who let in the Greeks and brought about the fall of Troy. The irony of this exchange is noted by Chaucer: the fickle mob overrule Hector's opposition, and insist on the return of one who 'was after traitour to the town / Of Troye' (IV.204–5). Thus the betrayer of Troy is exchanged for the betrayer of Troilus; and indeed the similarity of the names of the prince and the city helps to underline the connection. On both the small scale and the large, then, the poem presents 'false worldes brotelnesse' (V.1832) as a matter of betrayal.

6. Character

An important aspect of courtly romance is its tendency to present its story at least partly in terms of the consciousness of its leading characters. Their processes of thought and feeling are taken to be of intrinsic value, and the meaning of the story is largely defined through those processes. To us, familiar with the novel, there is nothing surprising in this; indeed the danger is rather than we may too easily take it for granted. It had not been so in the earlier heroic poems, where the characters had been seen through the external drama of their deeds and speeches, and story and meaning had scarcely begun to exist as separate categories. In French literature, a change came with the development of courtly romance and the introduction of self-analysis in the form of soliloquy. But English secular literature was little affected by this change before Chaucer's time: in one of the best pre-Chaucerian romances, *Ywain and Gawain*, which is translated from a major twelfth-century French romance, most of the French poet's psychologizing of the action is omitted, and only an exciting adventure story is left. It is not till the late fourteenth century, in the work of Chaucer and the *Gawain*-author, that we find English romances which focus sharply on their characters' consciousness and show them imagining how others must be thinking and feeling about them. 'Character' in romance is essentially consciousness; and there may be a wide gap between the formal *descriptio personarum*, such as Chaucer inserts at V.799–833, and the realization of consciousness. We should not fall into the trap of supposing that human character 'is' one kind of thing, but that there are different ways of presenting it in literature, some closer to the objective truth than others. There is no objective truth about character; different ways of presenting it represent different ways of seeing it; and Chaucer's way may differ from ours. For example, in the classic novel character tends to be conceived in evolutionary terms. People are thought of, certainly, as having some innate character-traits, but their characters undergo a process of development under the influence of external circumstances and social relationships. A typical kind of novel becomes the fictional biography or autobiography, such as *The Mill on the Floss* or *David Copperfield*.

We may take for granted this way of conceiving character, but it was not the medieval way. In Chaucer's England there was no autobiography or child psychology, and character tended to be seen as something fixed and not moulded by external influence. Thus, though the traitress Criseyde is the daughter of the traitor Calchas, Chaucer never shows the interest we might expect in the possible influence of her heredity and upbringing; for him, the interest of the fact is thematic, not psychological. Change of character Chaucer sees as a matter of instantaneous conversion rather than gradual development. An obvious example is Troilus's early change from scorner to devotee of love, a change corresponding to what *we* would see as a process of development in adolescence. Self-realization is another possibility, as when Troilus sees that he cannot 'unlove' the woman who has brought him such un-happiness (V.1695–1701). Such an internal event is conceived as virtually instantaneous, not as a lengthy process of '*coming* to see' something about oneself. On the other hand, though we may not think of the characters as gradually developing, it certainly happens that as the story proceeds we see them in changing lights. With Criseyde in particular, we are encouraged by the *slydying* nature of her speeches and the narrator's often baffled comments to see her now in one way, now in another. We cannot know for certain how medieval audiences reacted to this effect, but we are left to fit the different Criseydes together for ourselves, filling in the blanks left by the narrator's uncertainties.

Troilus

Chaucer began his work with a story, told in different versions, but always following the same unalterable outline. Character must have emerged as explanatory of story: what must we imagine the people to have been like, in order to explain how the story came to follow its course? That would not fix character—Chaucer's characters are significantly different from Boccaccio's—but it may help us to interpret it. In Troilus we have a character who is essentially passive before events. First, he is entirely dependent on Pandarus to arrange any contact with Criseyde. Later, when he is faced with separation from her, his passivity is stated as a conviction: Pandarus urges him to carry her off by force, but his objections to this conclude with what seems an even more fundamental reason than the need for secrecy to preserve her *name*: he cannot bring himself, 'though I deyen sholde, / To ravysshe hire, *but if hireself it wolde*' (IV.636–7). On this crucial point, he cannot conceive of doing anything but submitting his will to hers; and the result is disaster.

That was how it had to be, for there is no elopement in the old story; but we may suppose that Criseyde would have submitted with a good grace to being abducted, if she had been given no choice.

Troilus's submissiveness, then, is not merely a matter of literary or amatory convention: he is imagined by Chaucer not simply as the mouthpiece of a certain conception of love, but as the sort of person he would have to be, if he were truly committed to that conception. Diomede is perfectly capable of going through the motions of service and submission, though his real motto is 'He is a fool that wole foryete hymselve' (V.98); and Pandarus too is fluent enough in the language of love. Troilus is different; while others in his society—as no doubt in Chaucer's—pay lip-service to an idea of love, he really believes in it; what for them is literary convention or convenient pretence is for him a truth which he lives. This makes him a strange kind of person, and it would be wrong to suppose that Chaucer did not notice and intend this.

Many scholars would deny this. Kittredge wrote that 'The sufferings of Troilus are in complete accord with the medieval system. Lovers were expected to weep and wail, and to take to their beds in despair.' And C. S. Lewis described Troilus as simply 'an embodiment of the medieval ideal of lover and warrior'. Yet Charles Muscatine points out that 'It is difficult to think of a single hero of French romance who is quite so prostrated by love, so removed from the actual business of courtship, who depends so completely on an intermediary.'[1] Though medieval Englishmen probably wept more readily than is now customary, it remains true that Troilus makes a peculiar hero of a romance. E. T. Donaldson puts it amusingly:

> It is frequently said that Troilus is a typical courtly lover, but this can be true only in the sense that he could figure as the speaker of a brief Provençal lyric of unrequited love. But it is evident that when he is transferred into a high romance he has got himself into the wrong genre. Paralysis is all very well for under a hundred complaining lines, but more than eight thousand lines of hero's inaction do not leave us with much impression of heroism.[2]

The reference to lyric is helpful. Troilus has many speeches which could stand independently as courtly lyrics, quite apart from the actual songs he

[1] G. L. Kittredge, *Chaucer and his Poetry* (Cambridge, Mass. 1915), p. 123; C. S. Lewis, *The Allegory of Love* (Oxford 1936), p. 195; Charles Muscatine, *Chaucer and the French Tradition* (Berkeley 1957), p. 137.

[2] E. T. Donaldson, 'Chaucer and the Elusion of Clarity' (*Essays and Studies*, n.s. XXV (1972), pp. 23–44), pp. 33–4.

sings (one of them translated from a sonnet by Petrarch). Such speeches
tend to express single moments of paradox—or paralysis—but when a
character is conceived as actually living the part they imply, not at
isolated moments of intense emotion, but through all the practical details
of his life, he is bound to seem abnormal, and sometimes comically so.

Muscatine has noted how often comedy emerges from the
juxtaposition of Troilus with Pandarus. Troilus is not allowed to remain
passive and prostrate for long, without Pandarus rushing in, active,
plotting, cheerful, to provide a complete contrast, and to carry out for
him the practical actions for which his character unfits him. In the first
scene between them, Troilus appears to have fainted with grief, and
Pandarus bellows 'Awake!' at him, 'ful wonderlich and sharpe' (I.729);
to which Troilus, in a pained way, replies, 'Frend, though that I stylle lye,
/ I am nat deef' (I.752-3). Pandarus has earlier described Troilus as
'wallowing and weeping' like Niobe over her dead daughters; and this
undignified comparison both encourages us to see Troilus's grief
critically and provokes him to define a wilful element in it—'Ek I nyl nat
ben cured; I wol deye' (I.758). There are innumerable occasions when
we are incited to see Troilus's behaviour in a comic light. One notorious
example is the daring emphasis on the absurdity of Troilus's prostration
in Book III, right up to the moment when Pandarus has to push him into
Criseyde's bed and strip off his clothes. And there remain elements of
potential comedy even in Book V, and even in Pandarus's absence. There
is the string of questions Troilus asks himself (V.39-49) about why he
does not prevent Criseyde's removal—rhetorical questions, which are
left for the narrator to answer, in some embarrassment. On that occasion,
we are told that his manhood showed itself most fully in the fact that, for
once, he did not weep. Even later, Pandarus is again used to criticize
Troilus's excessive grief, when he remarks that it is only caused by a ten
days' absence, and that other knights have relinquished their ladies for a
whole fortnight without making 'halvendel the fare' (V.335). But by
now, as the inevitable end approaches, Pandarus's cheerfulness and
worldly wisdom are beginning to wear rather thin.

I do not mean to suggest that Troilus is merely a comic figure, and the
poem no more than an elaborate parody of courtly romance. Romances
not uncommonly include comic perspectives; and Troilus's situation is
fundamentally serious, and becomes increasingly so as the poem
proceeds. He has an exceptional capacity for suffering, which, for all his
readiness to fall into self-pity and despair, comes to demand our
admiration. In the loss and treachery of Criseyde, Troilus finds a cause
commensurate with his capacity for suffering, and in that sense achieves

fulfilment when most thoroughly frustrated. In Book V, as never before, the meaning of the action is fully carried in his consciousness. The stages of his passion, as he passes from anxiety through vain hopes to a nightmarish world of melancholy fantasies, an unending 'falle depe / From heighe o-lofte' (V.258–9) in which values themselves seem to dissolve into nothingness, are charted with unbearable clarity. There can be no question where our sympathies should be. Pandarus was right about Criseyde; but it is better to be wrong with Troilus than right with Pandarus.

Pandarus

Troilus's passivity makes it necessary for Pandarus's role to be active; and so, as a summarizing line puts it, 'He shof ay on, he to and fro was sent' (III.487). As with Troilus, Chaucer has not simply made Pandarus enact a role, but has imagined him as the kind of person who would so act by his very nature. Chaucer's Pandarus is a natural fixer, a man who enjoys bustling about, making practical arrangements, cheering people up, finding his own pleasure in managing others' lives. Chaucer has greatly increased the complication of his arrangements for bringing the lovers together, adding, for example, Troilus's imaginary soliloquy (II.523–39), the arrangement to lead Criseyde to the window as Troilus rides past, the deception of Deiphebus which permits a private meeting of the lovers at his house, the further deceptions which enable them to meet at Pandarus's own house, and all the elaborate machinery of curtains, trapdoors and cushions which must be set in motion to attain the goal. And Pandarus clearly takes delight in all these things, improvising joyfully when he has to, and caring only for his friends' happiness.

To be the manager of an illicit love affair, he must inevitably be a worldly man, and one who sees the world in a particular way. He sees it, without regret, as a realm of change, governed by Fortune with her ever-turning wheel. Troilus tends to regard Fortune as fixed and personal to himself—as destiny. But Pandarus stresses rather Fortune's impermanence and impersonality. In his view, one must accept her instability, and make use of her changes for one's own purposes. We would call him an opportunist, though he speaks not of opportunity but of *aventure*. He explains to Criseyde that

> to every wight som goodly aventure
> Som tyme is shape, if he it kan receyven;
> But if that he wol take of it no cure,
> Whan that it commeth, but wilfully it weyven,

> Lo, neyther cas ne fortune hym deceyven,
> But ryght his verray slouthe and wrecchednesse.
>
> (II.281–6)

And he uses the same argument when he is trying to persuade Troilus to prevent Criseyde's departure:

> Thenk ek Fortune, as wel thiselven woost,
> Helpeth hardy man to his enprise,
> And weyveth wrecches for hire cowardise.
>
> (IV.600–2)

But to seize the time is also to serve the time, and there is something of the time-server about Pandarus. His good nature makes him unwilling to press on a friend a disagreement or an unpalatable truth. When radical disagreement seems about to emerge, his impulse is to avoid it by saying, 'Yes, that's just what I mean.' Thus when he is trying to persuade Troilus to abduct Criseyde, and Troilus firmly replies that he will not, 'but if hireself it wolde' (IV.637), Pandarus, who has clearly not in the least intended that her consent should be asked, simply answers, 'Whi, so mene I . . . al this day' (IV.638). After this, Pandarus persistently fails to speak his true mind to Troilus, particularly about the likelihood of Criseyde's return. He tries to comfort Troilus with assurances that 'She nyl hire heste breken for no wight' (V.355); and yet, even before the ten days are up, we learn that he does not believe this. He expects everyone to serve the time as he does himself—Criseyde to betray Troilus once she has left, and Troilus to take a new mistress in her absence. It is telling that ultimately, when Troilus finds that he still cannot 'unlove' Criseyde, Pandarus has shifted ground, and helplessly exclaims that he hates her (V.1732). On the eve of the tenth day he is still giving Troilus false encouragement, and on the tenth day itself he continues, like the flatterer Placebo in *The Merchant's Tale*, to agree with what Troilus says, instead of speaking what he believes to be true:

> Pandare answerde, 'It may be, wel ynough,'
> And held with hym of al that evere he seyde.
> But in his herte he thoughte, and softe lough,
> And to hymself ful sobreliche he seyde,
> 'From haselwode, there joly Robyn pleyde,
> Shal come al that that thow abidest heere.'
>
> (V.1170–75)

Pandarus's brand of friendship, though undoubtedly based on a wish to make others happy, is shown to be corrupted by lack of principle. Medieval doctrines of friendship, which insist that 'the friend has the duty to advise and even rebuke when the occasion demands',[3] confirm this view; but any reader can see it for himself.

Pandarus's lack of principle should not surprise us, for it has emerged much earlier, in a different form, but also in the context of a wish to please. In Book I, to encourage Troilus to disclose the object of his love, Pandarus said that he would not keep him from the lady, 'theigh that it were Eleyne / That is thi brother wif, if ich it wiste' (I.677–8). A little later, he makes the same point with a different example: he would help him gain her, even if she were Pandarus's own sister (I.859–61). But in Pandarus the absence of principle goes along with strong scruples. He would be willing to procure for his friend his friend's sister-in-law or his own sister; but he is most anxious not to be thought of as a procurer, or at least not one who does it for money. Early in Book III, he feels guilt at what he has done to his niece in bringing her to the brink of becoming his friend's mistress. It is *shame*, he says, to mention what he has done for Troilus (III.249), and he cannot bring himself to utter the word for it:

> That is to seye, for the am I bicomen
> Bitwixen game and ernest, swich a meene
> As maken wommen unto men to comen;
> Al sey I nought, thow wost wel what I meene.
>
> (III.253–6)

If anyone knew what he had done, they would call it *trecherie* (III.278)—and thus he adds himself to the poem's growing list of betrayers—but at least he did it not for *coveitise* (III.261) but to abate Troilus's distress. The word that Pandarus has delicately omitted is 'bawd', as Troilus's answer indicates: 'me thoughte by thi speche / That this which thow me dost for compaignie, / I sholde wene it were a bauderye' (III.395–7). On the contrary, says Troilus, it should be called 'gentilesse, / Compassioun, and felawship, and trist' (III.402–3). And, to assure Pandarus that he really means those fine words, Troilus makes what is perhaps the poem's most shocking speech:

> I have my faire suster Polixene,
> Cassandre, Eleyne, or any of the frape,
> Be she nevere so fair or wel yshape,

[3] R. G. Cook, 'Chaucer's Pandarus and the Medieval Ideal of Friendship' (*Journal of English and Germanic Philology*, LXIX (1970), 407–24), p. 411.

> Telle me which thow wilt of everychone,
> To han for thyn, and lat me thanne allone.
>
> (III.409–13)

This might be less shocking on the lips of Pandarus, or of Diomede; but it shocks coming from Troilus, because it seems so uncharacteristic. It attempts a jaunty man-of-the-worldliness which comes with embarrassing awkwardness from the idealistic Troilus. Troilus nowhere else says anything so cold-bloodedly immoral, and, since it is translated directly from Boccaccio, one is tempted to say that it really belongs to the far less idealistic Troilo. But in fact the speech's incongruity is meant to be shocking, because it shows how near even Troilus is to being corrupted by his older friend's opportunism. Perhaps procuring for friendship is better than procuring for money; but the point of the exchange is that friendship, however genuine, if not based on principle, may be as corrupting as covetousness.

I have been stressing the more sombre aspects of Pandarus, almost to the exclusion of his endearing comic qualities, chiefly because the latter are more obvious, and cannot fail to get their due from any reader. His enjoyment of his part is infectious, whether in his jokes about his own lack of success in love, or his teasing affection for Criseyde after her first night with Troilus, when he hopes the rain has not kept her awake and made her head ache. And when his well-meaning schemes come tumbling down in ruins, there is genuine pathos in his helplessness, his inability to think of a single plan or even utter a cheerful word. His last words are, 'I kan namore seye' (V.1743).

Pandarus has been something of a voyeur: his fun has come from vicarious participation in that of others, and now that is no longer possible. But voyeurism is implicit in the very nature of the poem; and something can now be added to previous comments on the paradox of secrecy. The shared love-experience of Troilus and Criseyde is essentially private; but then what is the poet doing, evoking it so vividly that we seem to be present with them? Chaucer deals with this problem by making Pandarus, a character in the story, a substitute for himself as teller of the story. Pandarus from within does what Chaucer does from outside: cunningly manipulates events so as to bring the lovers together, and then stands aghast as a process beyond his control tears them apart again. Like the poem's narrator, Pandarus hops always behind in love's dance (II.1106–7), and compensates for this by taking an intimate interest in the young lovers. It is Pandarus who takes the narrator's place as witness of their first night together, sitting by the fireside, pretending to read an old romance, but always ready to step forward and give a push when necessary; and, if the audience feel inclined to snigger at the lovers' intimacies, they can express it openly through Pandarus before the consummation itself is described.[4]

Pandarus's first confident and then helpless acceptance that the world is a place of uncontrollable change also reflects the narrator's attitude. It is an easy step from Pandarus's comment on the exchange of prisoners—

> Swich is this world! forthi I thus diffyne,
> Ne trust no wight to fynden in Fortune
> Ay propretee; hire yiftes ben comune
>
> (IV.390–92)

—to the narrator's comment on the course of the whole story:

> Swich is this world, whoso it kan byholde:
> In ech estat is litel hertes reste.
> God leve us for to take it for the beste!
>
> (V.1748–50)

The only difference is that to the Christian narrator there is available the revelation of another world, while to the pagan Pandarus there is not. Pandarus and the narrator are not the same person; but in his conception of Pandarus Chaucer has gone far to establish as part of the poem's subject-matter the complex interaction between the reality of the story and the reality of the storytelling which is part of our experience, though usually concealed, of all works of fiction.

Criseyde

Nearly all readers, and especially male readers, find Criseyde the most fascinating and most complex of the poem's characters. She is made up of contradictory elements from beginning to end: an innocent widow, of uncertain age, who loves deeply and yet slips into treacherous infidelity. When Troilus first sees her in the temple, we are told:

> she stood ful lowe and stille allone,
> Byhynden other folk, in litel brede,
> And neigh the dore, ay undre shames drede,
> Simple of atir and debonaire of chere,
> With ful assured lokyng and manere.   (I.178–82)

[4] Cf. D. R. Howard, 'Literature and Sexuality: Book III of Chaucer's *Troilus*' (*Massachusetts Review*, VIII (1967), 442–56).

Everything seems in keeping with a picture of modest femininity, except the one word *assured*. The contradiction between shyness and self-possession immediately arouses interest. Her self-possession emerges at several points in the poem. Immediately after her entranced murmur of 'Who yaf me drynke?' (II.651) comes her cool, almost dispassionate consideration of the advisability of falling in love. In Book III, when Pandarus brings his story of how Troilus is distracted with jealousy, she asks him to take Troilus a ring, 'For ther is nothyng myghte hym bettre plese, / Save I myself, ne more hys herte apese' (III.886–7); and that sly (or innocent?) parenthesis 'Save I myself' raises many questions about how far she grasps the real situation, and how far she even perhaps intends that Troilus shall be thrust into her bed. Once she leaves Troy, the contradictions multiply. As she rides off with Diomede, bitterly unhappy, he makes a carefully calculated speech offering her his service. Her reception of it is just what is to be expected of a girl brutally parted from her lover: she has paid so little attention that its cunning has been wasted on her. But the next stanza says:

> But natheles she thonked Diomede
> Of al his travaile and his goode cheere,
> And that hym list his frendshipe hire to bede;
> And she accepteth it in good manere,
> And wol do fayn that is hym lief and dere,
> And trusten hym she wolde, and wel she myghte,
> As seyde she; and from hire hors sh'alighte.
>
> (V.183–9)

That implies a response so different that *natheles* will scarcely accommodate it. If she heard little of Diomede's speech, how could she answer it so elaborately? Was there any need to say, even in politeness, that she would 'do fayn that is hym lief and dere'? Can it be wondered that Diomede is encouraged by her reply to summon up his resources for a real attempt on her fidelity? Yet somehow we are convinced that there are answers to the many possible questions about Criseyde's motives.

This conviction is achieved by two means in particular. One is that, especially in Book II, Chaucer realizes Criseyde's own consciousness with unparalleled delicacy and subtlety. She sees Troilus ride past, and the sight makes its deep impact on her; then she is left alone with her thoughts, which are traced out in all their variability and contradictoriness with marvellous insight; then she wanders into the garden, and hears Antigone's song in praise of love, which sets off further trains of thought; then, as night falls, she goes to bed, hears a nightingale singing in the moonlight, and has her dream of the white eagle that painlessly claws out her heart and replaces it with his own. Chaucer has greatly expanded on the *Filostrato* here: the evocative outer setting, the song, and the dream are all new. In the extended sequence thereby produced, inner and outer experience influence and dissolve into each other, and finally Criseyde's waking thoughts and feelings, the lovely song, the falling darkness, the moonlight, and the nightingale's 'lay/ Of love' (II.921–2), all fade into the meaning-charged mystery of the dream. Is the dream a symbolic expression of her own wishes and fears, or a prophetic vision, or both? We are not told, and are left with our own thoughts, brought as close to the very texture of another person's consciousness as anywhere in literature.[5]

The other means of conviction relates to the narrator's role. I have suggested that an artistic function of the Chaucerian narrator's uncertainty and embarrassment is to engage our own imaginations in the creative work. This is so even in the dense sequence just discussed, where, after Criseyde has retired to her bedchamber, he adds:

> Whan al was hust, than lay she stille and thoughte
> Of al this thing; the manere and the wise
> Reherse it nedeth nought, for ye ben wise.   (II.915–17)

Our own wisdom must be called into play; still more so later, when we have to try to understand Criseyde's second 'conversion', from fidelity to infidelity. In Book V especially, the narrator is reluctant to say what Criseyde did and unable to say why she did it. From as early as the fourth proem, where he says that he must recount 'how Criseyde Troilus forsook', and adds 'Or, at the leeste, how that she was unkynde' (IV.15–16), he is anxious to protect her against too hasty or severe a judgment. When she assures Troilus that she will manage to deceive her father, the narrator insists,

> And treweliche, as writen wel I fynde,
> That al this thyng was seyd of good entente;
> And that hire herte trewe was and kynde
> Towardes hym, and spak right as she mente,
> And that she starf for wo neigh, whan she wente,
> And was in purpos evere to be trewe:
> Thus writen they that of hire werkes knewe.

(IV.1415–21)

[5] See further D. R. Howard, 'Experience, Language and Consciousness: *Troilus asnd Criseyde*, II, 596–931', in *Medieval Literature and Folklore Studies*, ed. J. Mandel and B. A. Rosenberg (New Brunswick 1970), pp. 173–92.

And yet we must wonder, who are these authorities knowledgeable enough to be able to interpret Criseyde's inward intentions? In Book V such references to the sources come thick and fast: 'as men in bokes rede' (V.19), there was no woman so reluctant to leave a town as Criseyde to leave Troy; 'the storie telleth us' (1037) that she gave Diomede a bay steed and a brooch given her by Troilus, and that 'Ther made nevere woman moore wo / Than she, whan that she falsed Troilus' (1051–3); men say (but Chaucer does not) that, besides the other presents, she gave Diomede her heart (1050); 'non auctour' tells us how long it took for her to forsake Troilus for Diomede (1088). As the final book proceeds, the focus gradually comes to rest in Troilus's consciousness, and Criseyde recedes and becomes incomprehensible, for Troilus and for the narrator too. To Troilus, Criseyde communicates only in letters, shifty documents attempting to conceal her motives from herself as well as from him. And when the narrator is not referring us to others' opinions, and thereby encouraging us to form our own, he persists in putting the best construction he can on what little information he has: even her last and shiftiest letter was written 'for routhe— / I take it so' (1587–8).

There is, then, a real mystery in Criseyde; she is a mystery even to herself; and Chaucer's narrative method encourages us to realize that mystery without ever dissolving it. In that sense, though we may speak of the characterization of Criseyde, we can hardly speak of her 'character', which has been seen by different critics in radically different ways. Thus C. S. Lewis saw her in Aristotelian terms, her single tragic flaw indicated by Chaucer's statement that 'she was the ferfulleste wight / That myghte be' (II.450–51); but D. S. Brewer has argued more recently that she possesses a self-confidence 'that triumphs and is fatal'—fatal in making her think herself able to keep her head in a love affair, despite her awareness that love is 'the mooste stormy lyf . . . that evere was bigonne' (II.778–9), and in making her think that she will be able to return to Troy once she has left.[6] There seems no way of settling such disagreements, because there is evidence in the poem for both views of Criseyde, and there is also ample stimulus for each reader or listener to create his own Criseyde—'Take every man now to his bokes heede' (V.1089).

[6] C. S. Lewis, op. cit., pp. 189–90; D. S. Brewer, 'Troilus and Criseyde' in The Middle Ages, ed. W. F. Bolton (London 1970), pp. 195–228, p. 216.

7. Feminism

The interpretation of Criseyde's character leads into a larger question of the attitude the poem expresses towards women. One formative factor in the development of courtly romance was probably the emergence of a courtly audience in which women played an important part. Much of the content of the romances, especially in their focusing on love as intense psychological experience, must have been intended to appeal to female listeners; and in the late fourteenth-century English court this was still the case. Chaucer specifically begs 'every lady bright of hewe, / And every gentil womman' (V.1772–3) not to be angry with him because his heroine was false. Yet in medieval society most real power was held by men, and there was a strong vein of misogyny in ecclesiastical thought, dominated as it was by a celibate male clerical class. So it is not surprising that the usual moral drawn from the story of Troilus and Criseyde was that of Boccaccio—

> . . . if you read with right feeling, you will not easily put your trust in all women. A young woman is inconstant and desirous of many lovers, and she rates her beauty more highly than does the mirror, and has exulting pride in her youth. . . . Ever unsteady as a leaf in the wind, she cares not for virtue or reason. . . . (124)

—or the more vehement version of the same view expressed by the author of the English alliterative poem, *The Destruction of Troy*.[1]

Chaucer's moral is different. In his conclusion he addresses not young men only, to warn them against female fickleness, but 'yonge, fresshe folkes, *he or she*' (V.1835), to warn them against all 'worldly vanyte' (V.1837). We have seen his anxiety throughout Book V to shield Criseyde from harsh or even objective appraisal, and to defend himself against any charge of being responsible for her treachery. His anxiety arouses suspicion, and we may even look for concealed meanings in his defence of his heroine: he will not chide her 'Forther than the storye wol devyse' (V.1094), yet surely that is far enough to condemn her; and he

[1] Ed. D. Donaldson and G. A. Panton, Early English Text Society 39 and 46 (London 1866–74), lines 8055–61.

would excuse her if he could (V.1099), yet perhaps that only implies that no excuse is possible. The Prologue to *The Legend of Good Women*, probably Chaucer's next major work, may strengthen our suspicions, for it represents Chaucer as accused in a dream by Cupid of writing against the religion of love, by telling the story of Criseyde and thereby making 'men to wommen lasse triste' (F.333). His defence, suggested by Alcestis, who is mentioned in *Troilus and Criseyde* as an example of *trouthe* contrasting with Criseyde's treachery (V.1527, 1778), is that he wrote 'Of innocence, and nyste what he seyde', and that 'He ne hath nat doon so grevously amys / To translaten that olde clerkes writen' (G.345, F.369–70).

We may thus receive encouragement to see *Troilus and Criseyde* as a sustained exercise in irony, in which an 'innocent' narrator, entirely distinct from the real Chaucer, falls in love with his fictional heroine, defends her against the manifest moral implications of her actions, and fails to understand that any intelligent listener will necessarily condemn her. This has been a common recent view of the poem, set forth most persuasively, perhaps, by E. T. Donaldson.[2] Much is to be learned from it, and it is true that Chaucer usually represents himself in his poems as simpler than he really is, and that his explicit judgments can rarely be taken at face-value. But still, in emphasizing praise or blame, such a view distorts the poem's effect. There can surely be no doubt that, whatever the final verdict on Criseyde, Chaucer has made an extraordinary effort to *understand* her situation and experience, not only as an individual but as a woman. The Scottish poet Gavin Douglas wrote of Chaucer that 'he was evir (God wait) all womanis frend'; and indeed, throughout his work, Chaucer shows an exceptional interest in his feminine characters. This interest is at its height in *Troilus and Criseyde*, where, more perhaps than anywhere else in medieval literature, we see the situation of a woman through her own eyes.

Criseyde is shown as a woman alone in a man's world, herself besieged in a besieged city, relying successively on her uncle, her lover, and her 'protector', and always at the mercy not only of the physical dangers of wartime, but of the images that men project upon her, the masculine assumptions which, indeed, are inevitably part of her own self-consciousness. A woman loses her *name* if she is known to have sexual relations outside marriage, but a man does not, and the women 'that jangle of love' (II.800), killing reputations with their gossiping tongues, conspire to subordinate their own sex. A woman can kill a man by not responding to his love; a true woman will show *pitee*; 'Women ben wise

2 See *Speaking of Chaucer*, chs 4–6, and 'Chaucer and the Elusion of Clarity'.

in short avysement' (IV.936). The acceptance of such generalizations as universal truths puts any individual woman under irresistible pressure to conform to them; and we have already seen how feelingly Chaucer represents Criseyde's vulnerability, as her desire and fear are played on, first by Pandarus and then by Diomede. At times she sees her own lot as that of women in general:

> . . . we wrecched wommen nothing konne,
> Whan us is wo, but wepe and sitte and thinke;
> Oure wrecche is this, oure owen wo to drynke. . . .
>
> How ofte tyme hath it yknowen be,
> The tresoun that to wommen hath ben do!
>
> (II.782-4, 792-3)

The poem's many such references to betrayal committed against women are of course ironic, since the story tells of betrayal committed *by* a woman. But they are not merely ironic. Criseyde really is betrayed as well as betrayer—betrayed equally by the opportunism of Pandarus and Diomede, and by the idealistic submissiveness of Troilus, into a position of 'sovereignty' she cannot sustain. Partly, at least, her infidelity is shown as a consequence of 'The tresoun that to wommen hath ben do' by society itself.

Chaucer's sympathy for women is not solemn, and at the end he can jokingly urge 'wommen that bitraised be / Thorugh false folk' to 'Beth war of men, and herkneth what I seye' (V.1780-85). And he is no partisan in the sex war, because he does not believe that things could be otherwise. Men, with their need to idealize, may put women on pedestals and grant them sovereignty in play; but if women achieve a real sovereignty, it does not bring them happiness. The Wife of Bath is a comic example of this: by sheer force of personality, she has dominated five husbands in succession, and yet her favourite was the last and cruellest. A tragicomic example is Dorigen of *The Franklin's Tale*, who in her husband's absence rashly promises to love another man if he removes the rocks from the Breton coast. When the task is performed, and fulfilment of her promise is demanded, she sees no way out but suicide; but at last instinct leads her to abandon her independence, and to submit to her husband's direction. One element in Criseyde's tragedy, and in Troilus's too, is that masculine assumptions about love confer on her a power of decision which she has not the strength to use. Yet, men and women being what they are, there seems no alternative; and one of the kinds of inevitability that run through Chaucer's poem is that of the painful difference between the masculine and feminine points of view.

8. Beyond Romance

Realism

Much of this study has concerned *Troilus and Criseyde* as a romance, but I must conclude by discussing two opposite directions in which Chaucer moves outside the limits conventionally assigned to the field of romance. The first is the poem's movement towards realism. One common element in medieval romances was the fantastic and the excessive: impossibilities such as magic, giants, dragons, invincible weapons, and exaggerations such as heroes who kill thousands in battle, people of incredible beauty or ugliness, lions that suckle human children. The medieval sense of what was really possible may have differed from ours; but still, many things in medieval romances could not have been thought realistic by their original audiences, though they may well have been seen as having a symbolic bearing on real life. Fantastic stories, like fantastic dreams, may convey important truths. Chaucer apparently despised this aspect of romance, which indeed in English romances often takes a crudely materialistic form. He pays little attention to the most popular body of romance stories, the Arthurian legend, and his one poem that enters in any detail into the fantastic side of romance, *The Squire's Tale*, is attributed to an immature teller and left unfinished.

In *Troilus and Criseyde* Chaucer avoids all that is fantastic, and fits the events of his story into a supposedly historical setting, that of the Trojan war. A contemporary reader, Thomas Usk, praised Chaucer for his avoidance of 'any maner of nycete of storiers imaginacion',[1] and closer examination suggests that this avoidance was deliberate. Chaucer was perhaps consciously setting himself to write a romance that would stand apart from all English predecessors: one that would belong to a more mature European tradition, and would be fit to kiss the footsteps of 'Virgile, Ovide, Omer, Lucan, and Stace' (V.1792). We have seen how

---

[1] ('Any kind of foolishness of storyteller's imagining'.) *The Testament of Love*, ed. W. W. Skeat, *Chaucerian and Other Pieces* (Oxford 1897), III.iv.

its hero is defined not as the best but as the second best knight of Troy. On one occasion when we are told instead that he was second to none there is a significant reservation—'Al myghte a geant passen hym of myght' (V.838)—the best, that is, in the real world, if not in that of fantasy. A similar joke at the expense of the romance-fantastic is found when Criseyde says she will send Troilus a ring to calm his jealousy, and Pandarus answers,

> Ye, nece myn, that ryng moste han a stoon
> That myghte dede men alyve maken;
> And swich a ryng trowe I that ye have non.
>
> (III.891–3)

Healing rings are common properties in romances, but have no place in the real world represented here. And when Pandarus, having got the lovers safely into the same bed, turns to the fireside, 'And took a light, / As for to looke upon an olde romaunce' (III.979–80), the contrast between love as really experienced and love as read about in books is underlined. Throughout *Troilus and Criseyde* there runs a counter-pointing of romance and reality, implied for example in another reference to a book, when Pandarus finds his niece listening to 'the geste / Of the siege of Thebes' (II.83–4). They have just reached the point where 'the bisshop, as the book kan telle, / Amphiorax, fil thorugh the ground to helle' (104–5)—a patent absurdity, belonging only to fiction. And at times, even when following the superlative convention of romance, the poem does so in a way which contributes to its realism. Thus the description of the feast at Sarpedoun's house (V.435–48) tells us that everything—food, music, dancing ladies—was the best that could possibly be; only the following lines ask, 'But what availeth this to Troilus, / That for his sorwe nothyng of it roughte?' (V.449–50) To him, compared with the reality of his grief, it is a mere fantasy.

Troilus and Criseyde's psychological realism and the realism of much of its language have been sufficiently considered already, but something should be added about its material realism. Chaucer imagined the material setting of his story in fully realistic terms, and, though he takes a scholarly interest in the pagan and 'classical' details of his story, adding details such as 'a relik, heet Palladion' (I.153) and 'pleyes palestral' (V.304), his realization of events and setting is largely a matter of 'medievalization'. He imagines Troy as a city like his own London, enclosed in walls with gates in charge of a warden (Chaucer himself was living in a house over Aldgate when he wrote the poem), full of churches and noblemen's palaces, liable to 'smoky reyn' (III.628), with a river running through it like the Thames. In many scenes the everyday medieval setting is closely documented. A good example is Pandarus's visit to Criseyde to deliver Troilus's letter (II.1093–1302). He arrives early in the morning, and is taken up to her *chaumbre*, whence they descend into the *gardyn* for greater privacy. When Criseyde says, 'Go we dyne', they return inside, to the *halle*. There she leaves Pandarus while she retires to her *chambre* again with 'some of hire wommen', to read the letter. She returns to the hall, and finding Pandarus deep in thought, laughingly seizes his hood. 'Tho wesshen they, and sette hem down, and ete', and 'after noon' Pandarus 'Gan drawe hym to the wyndowe next the strete', under the pretext of asking who has redecorated the house opposite. Left alone once more, they sit in the window seat, and he asks whether she liked the letter, and urges her to write an answer. She retires into a *closet* to do so, then returns to Pandarus,

> Ther as he sat and loked into the strete,
> And down she sette hire by hym on a stoon
> Of jaspre, upon a quysshyn gold-ybete.
>
> (II.1227–9)

As Pandarus had planned, Troilus now appears 'at the stretes ende'. Pandarus urges Criseyde not to leave the window lest she seems to be avoiding him; the young people blush as a glance is exchanged; and Troilus rides away home. Pandarus and Criseyde continue talking, and, at last, 'whan that it was eve, / And al was wel, he roos and tok his leve.'

The passing of time, and the characters' movements from place to place, as well as their shifting awareness and unawareness of each other, are documented with great accuracy; and, though *we* may find something exotic in the jasper pillar and gold-embroidered cushion, these were modern luxuries to Chaucer's audience. Through such scenes, where familiar encounters of friends and relations take place in an everyday world of houses and rooms, curtains and cushions, Chaucer creates the sense of a medieval society behind the foreground of personal action. The society, as we have seen, is limited as to social class (though little more so than in Jane Austen's novels), and Chaucer's picture of it is also limited in giving nothing of its economic structure, of where the money comes from or who does the work. But, within these limits, Chaucer's realism is complete and satisfying.[2]

Yet, in another sense, realism can never be complete. The simplest reality is infinitely rich and complex, and the poet must inevitably select

---

[2] On tendencies towards realism in romance, see Rosemond Tuve, *Allegorical Imagery* (Princeton 1966), pp. 336ff.

one detail rather than another. In doing so, he becomes something other than a mirror or a camera; and Chaucer, unlike many novelists, does not attempt to conceal this, or to pretend that his fiction is a world complete in itself. Sometimes, indeed, he will seem to bring us into direct contact with a real world, complete both materially and psychologically; but then he deliberately shatters the illusion, and reminds us that he is only using words. So it is with the scene in Deiphebus's house beginning towards the end of Book II. As Troilus lies in bed there, waiting tensely for his first meeting with Criseyde, Chaucer brings the book to an end with a question that invites us to imagine the sequel. Then comes the entirely separate seven-stanza proem to Book III, and only after this tantalizing gap does Chaucer return to Troilus. We have been forcibly reminded of the poetic artifice which both makes and unmakes the illusion of reality. Then the illusion is resumed for some four hundred lines more of detailed narration; this passes almost imperceptibly into a summarizing narrative of a *proces* (III.470) lasting some time, of exchanged messages and hasty meetings; and then once more the poet intervenes:

> But now, paraunter, som man wayten wolde
> That every word, or soonde, or look, or cheere
> Of Troilus that I rehercen sholde,
> In al this while unto his lady deere.
> I trowe it were a long thyng for to here;
> Or of what wight that stant in swich disjoynte,
> His wordes alle, or every look, to poynte.
>
> For sothe, I have naught herd it don er this
> In story non, ne no man here, I wene;
> And though I wolde, I koude nought, ywys;
> For ther was som epistel hem bitwene,
> That wolde, as seyth myn autour, wel contene
> Neigh half this book, of which hym liste nought write.
> How sholde I thanne a lyne of it endite?

(III.491–504)

Nothing could show more clearly than this apology Chaucer's awareness of the limits of realism, not just in his own narrative but in fiction in general. And the stanzas actively create in us the awareness they express, as Chaucer breaks the fictional illusion to remind us that no fictional illusion can be total. The process and dilemmas of writing are not suppressed but are incorporated into the poem written, so that, even as we read it, we are kept aware of the nature and limits of its art.

Philosophy

The other respect in which *Troilus and Criseyde* transcends the normal limits of romance is in being a philosophical poem. French courtly romances had contained an interpretation of meaning (*sen*) as well as a sequence of adventures, and in some, indeed, the *sen* had expanded so far as to amount to a continuous allegorical interpretation. Most English romances, however, had shown more interest in adventures for their own sake, and had left meaning to emerge with little guidance from storyteller or characters. Chaucer, in a single step, had gone beyond this, and invented a new category, of 'philosophical romance'. Within this category, which later included *The Knight's Tale* and *The Franklin's Tale* as well as *Troilus and Criseyde*, the poet not only showed what motives and values influenced the characters' actions and provided criteria for judging them, but went on to explore the nature of the world in which such events could occur. The content and terminology of such enquiries were provided largely by the *De Consolatione Philosophiae* of the sixth-century Latin writer Boethius, which Chaucer had himself translated only a few years earlier. Boethius's work consists of a dialogue, in which he—imprisoned, and shortly to be tortured and executed—protests against the loss of his former happiness, and against all the other misfortunes of earthly life, while Philosophy shows him that such things are not incompatible with God's providential order. The *De Consolatione* also takes up such topics as earthly honour and its mutability, and the spreading of divine love through the universe, which we have seen to be among the themes of Chaucer's poem. Chaucer added to the *Filostrato* over twenty passages derived from Boethius. These vary in importance from brief allusions to large-scale borrowings, such as Troilus's song in praise of love (III.1744–71) and his soliloquy on predestination (IV.953–1085). Most of the Boethian additions of any length concern two connected philosophical themes: Fortune, and predestination and free will.

Fortune is the figure, imagined as a fickle woman constantly turning a great wheel, who stands for those elements of change and unpredictability that lie outside the individual's control and form a central part of his experience of life. The image derives from Boethius, but the concept was widespread in medieval thought, with its emphasis on the unreliability of all earthly things, and was already present in the *Filostrato*. Fortune underlies the medieval conception of tragedy, for, as Boethius wrote, 'What other thyng bywaylen the cryinges of tragedyes but oonly the dedes of Fortune, that with unwar strook overturneth the realmes of greet nobleye?' (*Boece* II, pr. 2, 67–70) This, rather than any more recent conception, must be what Chaucer has in mind when he calls his poem a *tragedye* (V.1786): it emphasizes the sufferings that come upon men through the action of external forces, rather than that destructive and self-destructive energy, inextricably involved with the hero's greatness, that we may find in Shakespeare or Racine. From a modern point of view, the dominant effect of Chaucer's poem is perhaps pathos rather than tragedy—which does not imply failure, only difference.

The attitudes of the poem's characters towards Fortune vary significantly. In his first sorrow, Troilus exclaims that Fortune is his foe (I.837), while Pandarus replies that Fortune is 'comune / To everi manere wight', that she would not be Fortune if 'hire whiel stynte any thyng to torne', and that therefore sorrows as well as joys must pass (I.841–54). Troilus's sorrow does pass, with Pandarus's help; and indeed Pandarus's opportunism is an attempt to *use* Fortune for his own purposes. Fortune is responsible for the happiness of fulfilled love and, by implication, also for its brevity, for she grants any state only for 'a tyme'—'And thus Fortune a tyme ledde in joie / Criseyde, and ek this kynges sone of Troie' (III.1714–15). When Troilus's joy in turn passes, with the loss of Criseyde, that too is the consequence of Fortune's turning wheel, now seen as positively malicious: 'And whan a wight is from hire whiel ythrowe, / Than laugheth she, and maketh hym the mowe' (IV.6–7). Now Pandarus, apparently forgetting his earlier argument, asks, 'Who wolde have wend that in so litel a throwe / Fortune oure joie wold han overthrowe?' (IV.384–5), and has to remind himself that 'hire yiftes ben comune' (392). Pandarus similarly adopts contradictory attitudes towards Fortune when he first warns Troilus, at the height of his happiness, to do nothing himself to bring it to an end,

> For of fortunes sharpe adversitee
> The worste kynde of infortune is this,
> A man to han ben in prosperitee,
> And it remembren, whan it passed is,
>
> (III.1625–8)

and then is bitterly reminded of this by Troilus (IV.481–3) when Pandarus tells him that it is better to have enjoyed love and lost it than (like himself) never to have had it. Pandarus may think he can master Fortune, and may urge Troilus to do the same (IV.600–2), but it cannot be; nor is it better to worship Fortune, for she cannot be placated, as Troilus finds:

> Fortune, allas the while!
> What have I don? What have I the agylt? . . .
> Have I the nought honoured al my lyve,
> As thow wel woost, above the goddes alle?
>
> (IV.260–1, 267–8)

Fortune, though, is not merely a false deity worshipped by pagans; she is the ruler of the world itself, 'as it is hire comitted / Thorugh purveyaunce and disposicioun / Of heighe Jove' (V.1542–4), bringing about the fall of Troy as well as the misery of Troilus. She is the personification of 'Swich is this world', for Christians as much as for pagans.

Troilus, the poem's deepest thinker, goes beyond Fortune to consider free will and predestination. His soliloquy in Book IV closely follows Boethius (V, pr. 2 and 3), but is intimately related to the poem's thought on Fortune, and to fourteenth-century philosophical interests in general. If men are totally at Fortune's mercy, then, even if divine providence stands behind Fortune, their freedom of will must surely be illusory. This is the conclusion Troilus reaches; and that is in keeping with his tendency towards passive submission, towards seeing the sources of activity as external to himself. Usk, indeed, regarding Chaucer as 'the noble philosophical poete in Englissh', asserted that in *Troilus and Criseyde* he had solved the problem of predestination and free will; twentieth-century scholars, however, have tended to argue that, since Chaucer makes Troilus omit Boethius's final demonstration that free will exists after all, he must have expected his audience to recognize the omission, and to realize that Troilus, as a pagan, was in error. It is unlikely that Chaucer could rely on having such scholarly listeners; and in any event there was a notable predestinarian tendency in the Christian thought of his time. Thus Thomas Bradwardine, who ended as archbishop of Canterbury, explained the origin of his major work, the *De Causa Dei*, as lying in his revulsion against the voluntarist doctrines of early fourteenth-century Oxford. Against these doctrines Bradwardine developed a predestinarianism which, it has been said, 'in the extremity of its views, . . . went far towards the position taken by Luther and Calvin in the sixteenth century.'[3] Whether or not Chaucer shared Bradwardine's views, that the question was still controversial is shown by many references to it in contemporary vernacular literature, including, for example, *Piers Plowman*.

In including Troilus's soliloquy, then, Chaucer was responding to a strong current of interest in his own time; but the passage's deepest

---

[3] Gordon Leff, *Bradwardine and the Pelagians* (Cambridge 1957), pp. 11–14.

relevance to the poem's subject-matter once more relates to the experience of composing and receiving the poem itself. The outcome of the story was literally predetermined in that it came from authoritative and unalterable sources. 'Thus to ben lorn' (IV.958) *was* Troilus's destiny, not because the predestinarians were right about the world, but because he was a character in this story. Yet Chaucer confers on his characters a powerful sense of free will; we have seen how this is achieved, for example at Criseyde's two crucial moments of decision (whether to love Troilus and whether to leave him), partly by an intense realization of the characters' consciousness, and partly by separating off one segment of time from another, so that each seems undetermined present as it swings from future to past. Chaucer's own experience as writer must have brought before him particularly strongly this dilemma of his time; and he in turn brings it before us as we respond to his poem's movement through its time and ours. I greatly doubt whether he intended to offer a solution to the fundamental philosophical problem; his achievement was to re-create a dilemma which, as a writer, he had lived, rather than to solve it.

Is *Troilus and Criseyde*, then, philosophically coherent? The major difficulty has been found in its treatment of the theme of love. We have seen that Chaucer is not content to praise love as a human value and to deplore its failure. In Book III, both the proem and Troilus's song celebrate human love as an aspect of the divine love that governs the universe; and yet, by the end of Book V, both Troilus and the narrator have changed their positions radically. In another addition to the *Filostrato* which is absent from certain manuscripts (taken this time from another of Boccaccio's poems, the *Teseida*), Troilus, after his death in battle, is carried in soul up to the heavens. There he despises

> This wrecched world, and held al vanite
> To respect of the pleyn felicite
> That is in hevene above,
>
> (V.1817–19)

laughs at those weeping for his death, and condemns 'al oure werk that foloweth so / The blynde lust, the which that may nat laste' (V.1823–4). There has been much controversy as to the significance of this addition; has Troilus, as some thought possible for a good pagan, achieved salvation? Is his a Christian vision of the relation between earthly and heavenly values? It is even uncertain which of the heavenly spheres is the scene of his vision, and which the ultimate destination of his soul. Perhaps no definitive answers are possible to these questions; perhaps none are meant to be possible. But the immediate effect of the passage is unquestionably one of shock at an abrupt transition from an earthly to a heavenly point of view. There can be no reconciling the perspective of those below, weeping for Troilus's death, with that of Troilus above, laughing at their grief. The chain linking earth with heaven seems to have broken, and the break is what justifies the shift in the narrator's position, as he distinguishes sharply between the earthly and heavenly loves that he had earlier identified. It is not philosophical coherence that is aimed at here, but poetic and dramatic coherence.

It seems likely that Chaucer and his audience lived in two worlds of thought and feeling: one, that of the secular culture of their time, which saw human love as a real good, though inevitably, like the culture itself, a transient good; and the other, that of the religious doctrine to which on the deepest level they were genuinely committed, and which could find no place for any merely human love as a good at all. The split between the two is acted out in Chaucer's Retractions at the end of the *Canterbury Tales*, where he divides his writings into two groups, one of religious and moral works which he is glad to have composed, and the other of secular works which he renounces. At the head of the two groups stand, respectively, *Boece* and *Troilus and Criseyde*; and this alone should prevent us from trying to see the *Troilus* as substantially an exposition of Christian doctrine. The best that could be hoped for, in a truly serious poem about human love, was a movement from one world to the other; and this Chaucer achieves, with remarkable skill and conviction. The shock of Troilus's laughter from the heavens propels us towards a religious perspective; but that perspective is no novelty in the poem, for it has been prepared by the constant use of religious language to describe human love, and the repeated reminders of the existence of the Christian world of the storyteller and his audience alongside the pagan world of the story.

Chaucer is indeed a noble philosophical poet, but he is not a philosopher, and *Troilus and Criseyde* is a philosophical poem, not a philosophical tract. When philosophy is absorbed into poetry, its sharp definition begins to shift and blur; in *Troilus and Criseyde*, Boethian though much of it is by origin, the beautiful clarity of Boethius's argument is transformed into something richer and stranger, as it becomes part of a structure of feelings that are complex and even contradictory. Even as earthly values are renounced at the close, they are affectionately evoked in references to the earth as 'This litel spot . . . that with the se / Embraced is' (V.1815–16)—*embraced* touchingly recalls human love—and as 'a faire . . . that passeth soone as floures faire' (1840–41). Even 'the forme of olde clerkis speche / In poetrie' (1854–5) is subject to mutability; even Chaucer's poem is likely to be miscopied as time passes; and we have been warned earlier, in a larger perspective still, that 'in forme of speche is chaunge / Withinne a thousand yeer' (II.22–3). Chaucer has the keenest sense of the transitoriness of all earthly things; the shifting earth and our sliding human languages offer no firm standpoint from which to grasp at ultimate values. The poem's end, then, offers a final but not a total view of the meaning of its story. The essence of the work lies in movement, change; and the reader must move through it again and again, realizing it as a shape changing in time, and himself changing with it.

Further Reading

John Bayley, *The Characters of Love* (London 1960).

D. S. Brewer, 'Troilus and Criseyde', in *The Middle Ages*, ed. W. F. Bolton (London 1970).

'Honour in Chaucer', *Essays and Studies*, n.s. XXVI (1973), 1–19.

E. T. Donaldson, *Speaking of Chaucer* (London 1970).

'Chaucer and the Elusion of Clarity', *Essays and Studies*, n.s. XXV (1972), 23–44.

D. R. Howard, 'Literature and Sexuality: Book III of Chaucer's *Troilus*', *Massachusetts Review*, VIII (1967), 442–56.

'Experience, Language and Consciousness: *Troilus and Criseyde*, II, 596–931', in *Medieval Literature and Folklore Studies*, ed. J. Mandel and B. A. Rosenberg (New Brunswick 1970), 173–92.

R. M. Jordan, *Chaucer and the Shape of Creation* (Cambridge, Mass. 1967).

P. M. Kean, *Chaucer and the Making of English Poetry* (London 1972), vol.I.

John Lawlor, *Chaucer* (London 1968).

C. S. Lewis, *The Allegory of Love* (Oxford 1936).

Charles Muscatine, *Chaucer and the French Tradition* (Berkeley 1957).

Elizabeth Salter, '*Troilus and Criseyde*: a Reconsideration', in *Patterns of Love and Courtesy*, ed. John Lawlor (London 1966).

G. T. Shepherd, '*Troilus and Criseyde*', in *Chaucer and Chaucerians*, ed. D. S. Brewer (London 1966).

A. C. Spearing, *Criticism and Medieval Poetry* (London, 2nd edn. 1972).

Index